RADIATING CHRIST

Radiating Christ

An Appeal to Militant Catholics

From the French of

Raoul Plus, S.J.

IMPRIMATUR juxta Editionem ab

Ordinario Westmonasterii jam
approbatam.

✠ JOANNES A. FLOERSH

Archiepiscopus Ludovicopolita.

Ludovicopoli, die 2 mensis Octobris,
1944

ISBN# 1-891280-01-5

Library of Congress Number 98-070491

Copyright© 1998 CMJ Associates, Inc. Marian
Publishers

(This edition published under licence from original publishers)
Burns & Oates of Wellwood
North Farm Road, Kent TN2 3DR

Manufactured in the United States of America

CMJ Marian Publishers
P.O. Box 661, Oak Lawn, Illinois 60454

www.cmjbooks.com

INTRODUCTION

HOW TO RADIATE CHRIST

To be a "Christ" is the whole meaning of Christianity.[1] To radiate Christ is the whole meaning of the Christian Apostolate.

Everybody knows that the Christian is bound as far as possible to be a living "Christ," another Jesus Christ. How is he to do this? There are various books which will tell him: *In Christ Jesus;*[2] *Christ the life of the soul, by Abbot Marmion;*[3] and in a shorter form: *One with Jesus,* by P. de Jaegher, S.J.[4]

But to be a Christ for one's own personal benefit is not enough; we have to Christianize those around us; in a word, we have to radiate Christ. The following pages are intended to suggest to souls that are athirst

---

[1] "The aspect of the Catholic Religion which gives me such satisfaction is . . . the obligation of considering oneself a continuation of Christ, each of our lives making up for what He did not live on earth." Rene Schwob: *Ne Grec, ni Juif, p. 140.*

[2] By Raoul Plus, S.J. Published by Burns Oates & Washbourne Ltd.

[3] Published by Sands & Co.

[4] Published by Burns Oates & Washbourne Ltd.

for apostolic conquest, the means by which their apostolate may be made successful.

What method must we use in order to radiate Christ? Well, let us ask ourselves what method Our Lord Himself used to gain the adherence of His contemporaries. Antecedently it must be admitted that the means which He chose are the very means which I should do well to make my own. He, the Redeemer, possesses all the secrets of Redemption. Accordingly, however His methods may astonish or even scandalize me, if I see that He chooses this formula rather than that other, it is for me to submit to His judgment. His formula is certainly the good one; it must become my formula, too.

But it may be objected that Jesus Christ, the Head of the Body, possessed precious resurces which I, a mere member of that Body, do not possess.

Admittedly, Jesus possessed in His own right three qualifications which set Him entirely apart:

He was the Son of God.

He had at His disposal the power of miracles.

He had a personal charm beyond compare.

But surely, continues our objector, we must lose heart from the very beginning when we consider that Jesus so far surpasses us in resources for the conquest of souls. —Not at all. If we begin by contemplating what is beyond our imitation and set our divine Head on a pedestal infinitely beyond our reach, we shall inevitably take courage. Is it not well that the great Chief whom we serve is evidently and incomparably great? And when we see how high He stands, how brightly and clearly His power shines forth, are we not filled with a boundless confidence? When Jesus says: "Be of good heart, I have overcome the world," our hearts take courage; for we see that He who leads is a Person of a different calibre from us.

He is the sort of leader that we can march with. Under Him, victory is assured.

But let us hasten to add: if Christ, our divine eldest Brother, possesses means of supernatural conquest which belongs to Him alone, we must not forget that He often deigned to forgo the use of these weapons, to manifest them as little as possible and, almost under protest, that in a great number of cases He vouchsafed to appear to His contemporaries as if He were a mere man among men, endowed with nothing more than a human power. And to that extent, the example which He has given of the manner in which we should influence others retains its full value.

But we must say more. We must say that His divine technique in the supernatural conquest of the world must be our technique too.

What did Christ do in order to win His contemporaries? The Creed tells us, and we recite the words often, perhaps without understanding that they lay upon us a greater obligation than we think. It is all summed up in four phases:

Descendit de coelis;

Incarnatus est;

Passus;

Et sepultus est.

A descent, a descent from heaven;—the Incarnation;—the Cross;—the Burial.

Primarily and immediately these expressions have reference only to Our Lord. But, if only we understand them aright, they may easily be adapted to us also, and they wonderfully describe the only true means which any savior of souls must choose if his apostolate is to be effective.

The servant is not greater than his Master. Subordinate saviors cannot choose any other method than that of the principal Savior. And the rule which governs all apostolic action, all redemptive conquest, remains always that which Our Lord determined. Every apostle, If his work is to be fruitful, needs:

A descent, a coming down from heaven;

An Incarnation;

Renunciation;

Burial.

Our purpose is just to explain what this means. It means so many things! Things which only few people understand. And this is why there are so few genuine saviors of souls, so few people who, from God's point of view, exert real influence upon those around them.

But we may assert now from the very beginning, and as you read on you will become more and more convinced, that any method for the salvation of souls other than that of the Savior, is a fantastic creation of the imagination, an impossibility.

If you are not prepared to submit to the truth, then read no further.

CONTENTS

BOOK I

"Descendit de coelis."
DESCENT FROM HEAVEN

CHAPTER I

DESCENT

THE winning of souls calls in the first place for humility: descent. The first virtue that the apostle must have if he would influence his contemporaries is disinterestedness.

What is an apostle? Etymology tells us that he is one who is sent, *missus, αποστολος,* one who comes in the the name of another, who comes not to speak of himself, not to plead his own cause, but to speak of another, to plead the cause of another, another who is understood to be greater than himself; the apostle come to speak of God, to plead the cause of God.

In what terms does St. Paul explain the part that he and his fellow-laborers are to play in the apostolate? *Segragatus in Evangelium,* he says[1]: set apart to preach the Gospel. *Dispensatories mysteriorum Dei*[2]: dispensers of the mysteries of God. And, still more briefly, *Dei adjutores*[3]*;* God's helpers, God's fellow-workers. The apostles are not to preach themselves. No, not at all.

[1] Rom. i, I.   [2] I Cor. iv, I.   [3] I Cor. iii, 9.

Nos praedicamus Christum[4]; it is Christ that we preach; *pro Christo legatione fungimur*[5]; for Christ we are ambassadors. St. Peter's motto is the same: *Si quis loquitur, quasi sermones Dei*[6]: if any man speak let him speak as of the words of God.

And Our Lord Himself, in the Parable of the Sower, gives us to understand that he that goes forth to sow, is there to sow the *seed, seminare semen*; he has to cast the seed to the four winds, seed which is not something of his own substance, but which comes from without. If you sow human seed you will never get a divine fruit; only from the divine seed will the divine plant grow. And when the good Master sends forth His apostles to teach all nations and to baptize, He tells them that they are to do this "in the name of the Father and of the Son and of the Holy Ghost."[7]

What you distribute, He says to them, distribute gratuitously; *gratis date*, seeking no personal advantage or renown.

It is a wonderful thing that God should have made use of other men to address Himself to mankind; that He should not

---

[4] I Cor. i, 23.
[5] 2 Cor. v, 20.
[6] I Pet. iv, II.
[7] Matt. xxviii, 19.

have contented Himself with acting within the souls of men, in the intimate recesses of their consciences. It is a wonderful thing that Christ, to awaken human beings to the truth of the Gospel, should have vouchsafed to make use of "beaten air," to entrust His thought and His love to men, giving them the task of transmitting them to their brethren: *Fides ex auditu*; the great majority will come to the light of truth only by making use of the instrument of Providence, the preacher of the Gospel. "Jesus," wrote Peguy, "has placed Himself at a great disadvantage; he has placed himself at the disadvantage of standing in need of us."

They will be chosen men, it is true; God will carefully select the official ministers of the Word. He will fit them by a special training for their apostolic work; they will be qualified men. The Church will have a body of teachers whose official function will be to distribute the truth; they are the priests.

Meanwhile let us not fail to pay our tribute of admiration to this wondrous creation of Our Savior, the priesthood. What a difference there is between the priest and the layman! However marvelously the layman may be endowed, none of his actions can produce their effect *ex opere operato*. The layman may indeed be a channel of grace in a certain manner, by his devotion, his charity, his self-sacrifice, his self-denial. But what is this compared with the power of the priest, who by baptism can make God enter into the soul and by penance restore Him; compared with the power of the priest at the bedside of the dying? The layman may help prepare a soul for grace; he cannot confer it. The layman may help to dispose a soul for pardon; only the priest can grant absolution. . . .

This is not to say that the priest alone is commanded to be an apostle. No, the laity also, especially at the present day when vocations to the priesthood are so few in this country,[8] are called to work for the salvation of their brethren.

What qualities do they need especially for this work? In the first place they need the deep humility of the man who seeks not to publish himself, but strives to disappear entirely behind the One whom he wants to preach.

Look at St John the Baptist. Men came to

[8] France.

seek him, thinking that perhaps he was the Messias. No. He, John the Baptist, is not worthy to even loosen the sandals of the Master and Savior. "See," he says, "there is the Messias." And he points to a man clad in a *burnous*, who comes forth from the desert. It is to Him that he sends his hearers and his disciples: "He must increase, but I must decrease."[9] A wonderful example of disinterestedness.

Andrew had been privileged to approach the Lord; he tells his brother Simon: "We have seen the Messias." He does not add: "You need not go to Him; I will tell you all about Him." No, he invites Simon to come in person and see the Master: "He brought him to Jesus."[10]

It is not for the intermediary to seek his own advantage and glory. It is his duty to show the way to the Master, and then, to disappear.

Look at St Paul, what is his aim? To make Christ reach the measure of the perfect man, by gathering together as many disciples as possible for the Saviour, and by leading them to the highest possible degree of evangelical perfection. And what part does

[9] John III, 30. [10] John i. 42.

St Paul ask for himself in this enterprise? Work? Yes, decidedly. Glory? Not at all. *Nil scio nisi Jesum.* Paul is nothing. It is Jesus only that counts.

Better still, we have the magnificent example of Our Lord Himself, who shows us how disinterestedness can win souls. What does the Savior seek? He seeks to win love for His Father. For Him that is everything; He wants nothing else: The Father, the father, it is always of the Father that He speaks; so much so that one day Philip says to Him: "Lord, show us the Father." His mission is to speak to the world the words which the Father has committed to Him to speak to the world: "The Father is greater than I. . . ."[11] "The words that I speak to you I speak not of myself"[12]; and when the Apostles ask Him to teach them how to pray, Our Lord teaches them the Our Father. We might multiply texts to illustrate this; here are a few:

"The Son cannot do anything of himself, but what he seeth the Father doing."

"As the Father hath life in Himself, so he hath given to the Son also to have life in himself. And he hath given him power to do

[11] John xiv, 28. [12] John xiv, 10.

8

judgment."

"I cannot of myself do anything. As I hear so I judge . . . I seek not my own will but the will of him who sent me."

"The works which the Father hath given me to perfect, the works themselves which I do, give testimony of me that the Father hath sent me."

"I am come in the name of my Father."[13]

"He that sent me is with me; and he hath not left me alone. For I do always the things that please him."[14]

"I came not of myself, but he sent me."[15]

●　　●　　●　　●　　●

Hence the first condition of an effective apostolate is to work, not for oneself, but for God, for Christ.

But working for God, for Christ, may be understood in a thousand ways. The only good way is to love the cause you have espoused, and love it with all your heart.

Zeal, if it is to be truly zeal, must be a

[13] John v, 19-47.
[14] John viii,.29.   [15] John viii, 42.

passion, a noble sort of jealousy; *zelus ejus, zelus ignis atque flammarum*, a zeal of flame and fire. We must hunger and thirst after justice, we must be tormented at the thought of those who suffer: "I have pity on the multitude." Not a pity which is mere sentiment, mere words, but a pity which is active, genuine, and therefore effective. *Non verbo neque lingua, sed opere et veritate.* Not in word or in tongue, but in deed and in truth.

When souls appreciate that he who wishes them well is in the first place absolutely disinterested, and secondly is desirous of their perfection, then they allow themselves to be approached; they are won by warmth as a warm stream melts an iceberg. Anything else can be resisted; but you cannot resist a burning zeal, if the zeal, as we have said, is disinterested, and if it is, as we shall say later, enlightened.

Who can measure the good that was done, for example, through the ardent charity of a Pierre Poyet or an Antoine Martel. Poyet, unable to convert one of his companions at the Ecole Normal Supérieure, wrote: "Christ seemed to say to me this morning: 'It depends solely upon you whether this soul will be saved, whether it will believe in Me and love Me. Will your faith and your love be great enough to win it?' I trembled with terror before this responsibility: the salvation of a soul." And at another time: "I should like to be a generosity merchant, and I am looking for associates."

Antoine Martel, a brilliant graduate, professor of Slavonic literature at the University of Lille, in a paper on the subject of "Charity and the professional virtues," wrote as follows:

"To live charity means, above all, to have the spirit of service, the spirit that makes us ready to spare others pain and render them service, even though it may cost us a part of our own resources: money, time, health, intelligence, powers of action. We are one of God's hands: the hand that works from without, while the other acts from within. We can to a great extent remove from the hearts of our brethren that which obstructs their approach to God. The only thing that can deliver us from our obstinate human illusions is a long exposure of our hearts to the truths of the Gospel."

He reproaches himself with having to write on charity, instead of living it. And yet

what love he showed for his brethren! He
wanted to go back to Russia, where he had
already been for purposes of study. What
drew him to return? Was it curiosity, the
desire of learning? Above all it was "sympathy" in the best sense of the word, the desire
to suffer with those whose suffering he well
understood. . . . "I feel this great people suffering,"[16] he wrote, "and I think I should
rejoice to share its unhappiness, willingly to
endure the evils which it is forced to bear. It
is this, rather than the feeling that I should
be able to bring them any help or comfort. I
should be lost, powerless. Suppose that this
desire to share the sufferings of one who
suffers is an unmixed desire. What do you
think of it? From a strictly rational stand-
point it is absurd. And yet there is something in the human soul (not only in the
Christian soul) which says exactly what the
words mean etymologically: 'suffering with.'
This desire to share the suffering of one who
is in distress, may include that desire for
suffering which so many saintly souls have
had, simply because they knew that their
Beloved, Our Lord, had undergone martyr-
dom, that He continued to suffer in His
Mystical Body, that He 'was in agony until

---

[16] *Lettres,* Edition du Cerf, p. 172.

the end of the world.' Is this not a supreme proof of love?"

In this passage Martel touches upon the ultimate reasons for devoting oneself to the salvation of souls. We must love souls for three reasons especially: because every soul represents some (perhaps much) fruit of the Blood of Christ; because every soul is a factor (perhaps a very important one) in the coming of the kingdom of God; because in doing good to a soul we do good to Christ in His Mystical Body.

•　　•　　•　　•　　•

If it is truly not his own cause that he is pleading, but Gods then the apostle, precisely because he is sure of the truth which he preaches, because he is in firm and conscious possession of the formula of salvation, will assert that truth with calm. And nothing is more convincing than the apostle's calm and incompromising manner, his tranquil assurance, that absence of prevarication and inconsistency: "Thus it is, and not otherwise." And whatever you do or say not one iota will he change: "Let your speech be yea, yea, nay, nay." What is, is; what is not, is not. In this Our Lord was our great model.

We like people to assert, we like people who give the impression of sureness, so that if they say anything it means that this is so, and they will not go back upon it. There are so many that use shifts and evasions, trying to convey the impression of subtlety, but really being uncertain of themselves. You will not win adherents by cleverness; you may gain a concession, you will not win admiration.

Even when Jesus saw that He offended His hearers, yet He persisted in His statements. His message, the good tidings, came from above; whatever happened He would transmit that message intact; and, even though it may protest and refuse to submit, the world likes it so.

Many of the teachings of the Savior ran counter to the current opinions of the time; whether it was a question of the requirements of charity, the forgiveness of injuries, or the pardon accorded to repentance; whether it was a question of the predominance of the internal motive (the simple eye) over the soulless practice of external rites, or the danger of riches, or the pharisaical spirit, Our Lord never attenuated His doctrine. It was the same in the matter of the Real Presence, the eternity of the pains of hell, the doctrine of the strait way and the narrow gate. "This saying is hard," said many of His hearers, and went away. But see, on the other hand, the confidence of those who remained faithful; see how, when the hour came, they gave evidence of their attachment to this Master of unparralled assurance, even by the shedding of their blood.

And St Paul, after the example of his Master, knew how to be assertive when it was necessary. He had been accused of appealing to the resurrection of the dead, and on that account he was cited to appear before the Jewish Council. Did he attempt to evade the issue? On the contrary he faced it: "Men, brethren . . . concerning the hope and resurrection of the dead I am called in question." And his frankness, far from resulting in his downfall, gained him the favor of the multitude: "We find no evil in this man!"

Young people especially like courage. A young naval ensign had lost his rosary. "Whom does this thing belong to?" asked a comrade who had found it. "To me," replied the owner. Did they jeer at him, did he lose anything in their esteem? On the contrary. He became thenceforth the refuge of any of his comrades who happened to be in trouble.

Nobody admires the half-hearted giver. Our Lord did not. A judicious mixture of courage and cowardice is odious; what is neither hot nor cold, but tepid, He vomits out of His mouth.

"There is no giving into evil," wrote Claudel, "there is no giving into deceit. There is only one thing to do with what is evil, and that is to destroy it." And Vigny: "Any man who has ideas and does not form them into a complete system is an incomplete man." And Goethe, more briefly still: "If you have seen a man who is a complete whole, you have seen a great thing."

People like to see men, as they say, "all of a piece," that is, consistent. Why are they so rare? In the case of many of the baptized, to use the cruel saying of Henri Heine, "the waters of baptism dry quickly." What a pity and what a shame! The story is told that in the old days the Irish used to baptize their children with their arms out of the water, "so that the child might use his arms without scruple to strangle his enemy, to caress his mistress or to shake his dice." How many there are who act as though one or other part of their being had not been touched by the sacred waters! But what a joy on the contrary, to find a person who is truly one, fully logical and consistent, in whom all is marked with the baptismal seal!

"What is your name?" asked the Roman governor, Rictiovar, of the young Quirinus.

"My name? Christian is my name." Nor could they extract any other answer from him. He might have explained that his name was Quirinus. But he chose a better: *Christianus*.

"Are you a member of the sacred band? are you a follower of Christ?" I can imagine two answers,[17] one of them the bold, courageous reply: "Yes, of course I am!"; the other, the answer of the coward: "Well, you see how it is; somebody persuaded me, and I did not like to refuse."

We are familiar with this second reply: does it not recall the answer of a certain apostle, when he was accosted by a servant-

[17] We have young men particularly in mind. Indeed it is for them that these pages were first written. Each reader must draw his own conclusions according to his own particular case.

girl, on the night of Our Lord's arrest: "Thou also wast with Jesus of Nazareth.—But he denied, saying; I neither know nor understand what thou sayest."

Which of the two attitudes, the courageous or the evasive, is the more to be admired?

We may remark also that when Christ asserts His identity He makes no compromise: "Art thou the Christ, the Son of the Blessed God?—I am."[18] "I am," nothing more—that is enough.

"You call me Master and Lord. And you say well; for so I am."[19]

The apostle must imitate the Master. But in his uncompromising firmness, if it is to be convincing, there must enter no element of self. It is not the person who speaks, but what is said, that matters.

---

[18] Mark, xiv, 61, 62.   [19] John xiii, 13.

CHAPTER II

DESCENT *(continud)*

BUT while firmness on principles must be absolute, adaptiveness to individuals should be cultivated to the utmost.

Our Lord gave Himself to all: to children, to sinners (the Magdalene, Simon, the adulterous woman, those possessed by devils), to the timid (Nicodemus), to the discouraged (the disciples of Emmaus), to condemned criminals (the thieves on the cross). He showed no preferences, unless it were for the most distressed; He took the lost sheep upon His shoulders, He adapted Himself to all. It was in imitation of this model that St Paul became all things to all men that he might win them to Christ.[1] The good Master did not crush the broken reed, nor did He extinguish the smoking flax. When questions were put, He answered them; when they asked Him how to pray, He taught them.

Indeed you might say that He did nothing else but place Himself at the disposal of any who wished to ask Him a question or a favor. He never seemed to be in a hurry. It

[1] I Cor. ix, 22.

is difficult to open your heart to one who appears always to be preoccupied or busy. "Seeing the multitudes, he went up into the mountain. And when he was set down his disciples came unto him."[2] On another occasion: "Jesus going out of the house, sat by the seashore . . . and he went up into a boat and sat."[3] . . . "On a certain day . . . he sat teaching."[4]

What a lesson for us ! Sitting down was equivalent to saying: "See, I am at your disposal, I am entirely at your service. I am most interested in what you have to say to me." Georges Duhamel once wrote: "The majority of people seem to suffer from a sense of neglect; they are unhappy because nobody takes them in hand, nobody is ready to accept the confidences they offer." And Ernest Hello, more briefly: "The great glory of charity is to understand."

That is what is needed—the gift of understanding others, the spontaneous offer of help; engaging a person in conversation on indifferent matters for a few minutes, just to give him the chance to say what he wants to say but does not dare. René Bazin somewhere speaks of a peasant he knew, who

[2] Matt. v, 1.   3 Matt. xiii, 1-2.   [4] Luke v, 17.

every morning used to go out into the fields and listen to the corn growing. So we ought to be able to listen to the seed that is growing in men's hearts, help it sprout, break up the clod of earth which the seed is too feeble to penetrate; signify by a pressure of the hand, by a smile, a passing word, that we are at the service of another, ready to welcome him, to give him our attention, to help—in a word, to devote ourselves to him.

• • • • •

You may be defending God's cause, but remember that you are not its only champion. You must not try to do everything by yourself; and this is another way of practicing that disinterestedness which is so effective a weapon in the hands of the apostle.

If there was ever One who might have accomplished unaided the whole task of Redemption, surely it was Our Lord. What need had He of help? And yet, with an unparalleled humility, He chose fellow workers, He gathered His disciples around Him, not to pay court to Him, but because He wanted to ask of them this curious service: to help Him, the Master of the world, to save the world.

Often instead of going Himself to preach the word or to do good, He sent His disciples in His place. They would do as well as He; indeed sometimes, with His permission, they would do better. He promised it in so may words: "He that believeth in me, the works that I do, he also shall do; and greater than these shall he do."[5] Indeed He pushed His disinterestedness so far as to accept failure for Himself, allowing another to carry His programme into effect. He, Jesus did not succeed; He died crucified, defeated, with all His apostles in flight. The Holy Ghost must needs come to begin the evangelical conquest of the world.

The application to our own case is easy. We must submit to be assisted by others and not make ourselves the sole centre of beneficent activity; we must choose collaborators, give them work to do, like to see them succeed, like to see them succeed better then ourselves. Nothing is more admirable than such selflessness, perhaps because it is so difficult—and so rare.

It is an attractive form of self-denial to admit others to work with you; you should welcome others to work by your side, that

[5] John xiv, 12.

is, you should be pleased to have other forms of apostolic activity besides that form which you yourself favor. But also you should be prepared to admit that there has been devoted work done *before* your time, work which has not been without fruit.

The young are especially inclined-so wrapped up are they in their own form of apostolate-to be resentful or critical of those who do not share their own particular type of work. The scout will think that there is nothing like scouts, the X.Y.Z. organization will think that there is nothing like the X.Y.Zs; forgetting that in the Father's house "there are many mansions." Others are wont to imagine that before their time nothing was ever done. Did Our Lord despise the past? Far from it; He did not deny the the value of the Old Testament, though it was His task to found the New. He often appealed to it, He often quoted the Prophets. "I am not come to destroy," He said, "but to fulfill." Let this be our motto. Admittedly a new situation requires new treatment; of course it is easy, in one's enthusiasm for one type of work, to overlook the advantages of an earlier—or a neigh-boring—organization. But such narrowness of outlook runs the risk of antagonizing others. The apostle's soul has a vaster vision. He is enthusiastic for his own organization and his own methods; but he is able at the same time to recognize the advantage of the organizations which have existed in the past and which still exist today, side by side with his own. A passionate zeal is a conquering force, but only if it is broad-minded. A narrow mind or a narrow heart will never conquer others.

· · · · ·

The apostle is in the service of Christ. But what sort of service is it? A casual employment, a sporadic service, with intervals during which everything is left to go to rack and ruin—or a constant service which takes up every minute of our time?

Are there any holidays in the service of Christ? In other words, are there certain moments when the blood of Christ is inoperative, the redemption without effect? Surely, the Kingdom of God calls for help at every moment, souls are constantly in need of our aid, incessantly the blood of Christ cries to heaven.

You are not an apostle for only half an hour a day; during the period of a meeting, or under certain circumstances; you are an apostle all the time, for twenty-four hours a day, for sixty minutes an hour, for sixty seconds a minute. The apostle is not like Moliére's Maître Jaques, putting on one old smock after the other. The apostolate is the work of every moment; not always of the same sort at every moment, but the work of every moment.

Again let us consider the example of Our Lord. Not for a moment did He forget the purpose for which He came. Whether in the synagogue or in the Temple, in the boat or on the shore, conversing with the Samaritan woman or appearing before Pilate, with His Apostles or before His judges—He is filled always with the sense of His mission. "My Father worketh till now; and I work."[6] Christ worked incessantly. The great task of the salvation of the world is a continuous drama, without intervals. The sentence we have just read was uttered by Our Lord in answer to the pharisees who had accused Him of healing the sick on the Sabbath.

Every instant God gives us being and life; and at every instant grace presses us, *gratia urget nos*. Every instant souls stand in

[6] John v, 17.

need of us, every instant the Father wants us to glorify Him, every instant the Son asks us to help Him.

"Every day they ceased not . . . to teach and preach Christ Jesus." So we are told of the Apostles in the early days of the Church. The rule is still the same, and it is equally urgent. The occasion will not always call for the same sort of activity; there is an apostolate for the time of work and an apostolate for the holidays. But there is no holiday from the apostolate. The Father works without ceasing; so did Christ; so does the Holy Ghost within the souls of men, calling them and assisting them at every moment, though they know it not. So did the twelve; not a day passed without their preaching Christ, And so do all apostles who understand the meaning of their vocation.

"All the time, and with all my soul." That is the motto of the apostle.

● ● ● ● ●

The primary rule for every apostle is that he must be willing to disappear behind the Master whom he preaches.

DESCENT

We should add that the apostle must devote himself to humble tasks, he must be able, as they say, "to descend to details"; he must not be content merely to have great ideas; he must come down to the concrete and attend to humble realities.

This has always been the mark of great men. Before considering our great Chief let us hear a human leader of men. Lyautey was above all a man of action. He defined himself as "an animal of action." A man of great breadth of intelligence, but also, and above all, a mind essentially practical, and remarkably endowed with the capacity of adapting itself to reality. It is a good thing to conceive a plan; it is everything to put it into execution.

A few weeks after his arrival at Tonquin he writes: "What a change from France! How delightful to feel that one is no longer working in a void, making plans for transport which will never transport anything, and preparing conventional maneuvers. Now I am in immediate contact with reality."

He derives his information not merely from books, but also from men on the spot, even from the officer of lowest rank, from all

27

those who, as he puts it," are at grips with reality." Circulars, abstract orders, these need to be adapted, modified, corrected. He goes so far as to call ready-made regulations "one of his greatest enemies," and asserts that "in action as well as science, theories must be transformed to suit the requirements of events and facts." "It is by being on the spot," he says, "and by handling men and things that you learn your job."

And Christ, the greatest of all leaders, never disdains the smallest trifles: those slow advances and that patient attention to detail which is necessary to overcome obstacles, apparently insignificant but in reality of the highest importance.

See the care with which He chooses and prepares His Apostles. How carefully He studies the method of approach to be used for different individuals! Recall the episode of Nicodemus, of the woman of Samaria, of the Centurion whose son is sick. There is no place or opportunity which the Savior does not utilize. He converses as easily with Zacheus on his sycamore tree as with Nathanael under his fig tree, with Simon the Pharisee in his dining-room, as with the Samaritan woman by the side of the well, with the masters of Israel in the synagogue as with the paralytic under the pent-roof of the pool of Probatica.

And how wonderfully He adapts His method to the character of those with whom He is speaking! Sometimes it will be a question that He puts to obtain the answer He desires: "Whom do men say that I am?"—"Some John the Baptist, and other some Elias, and others Jeremias or one of the prophets."—"But whom do you say that I am?"—"Thou art the Christ, the Son of the Living God."

At other times it is a sentence that arouses curiosity, a paradox:

"I am come not to bring peace but the sword."

"He that would save his life shall lose it."

"If thy right hand scandalize thee, cut it off."

"Whatsoever ye shall bind upon earth shall be bound also in heaven."

"Whither I go you cannot come."

Sometimes, though rarely, there is a sudden outburst, in order to impress a lesson more deeply upon the minds of His hearers. The temple of God is to be respected; and so He drives out the sellers with scourges. Thus His hearers will remember the lesson: "My house is the house of prayer." Similarly, when He wants to confound hypocrisy: "Ye whited sepulchers!"

But ordinarily His voice is calm and measured. He speaks in simple and homely fashion. Sometimes His voice is stern. But at all times He adapts Himself to His audience.

But Jesus is not only at His ease with children, with the Twelve, with His own friends, Martha, Mary, Lazarus, and certain of His disciples. He speaks to everybody, as He meets them, be they officials, judges, adversaries; to every age and condition of men; He puts Himself within the reach of all; He says what has to be said at the moment, awaiting God's own time to say what remains to be said. "You cannot bear it now. . . . He that hath ears to hear let him hear." He will return to the subject later if need arises, and if circumstances permit; if necessary He will create those circumstances, provided His hearers show their goodwill and do not insist upon remaining deaf to His words.

When He knows that a particular doctrine is beyond the capacity of the masses, He asks His chosen ones to keep it to themselves for the present. To what purpose is it—in His own singularly forcible words—to place pearls before swine? Everything is not meant for all in the same degree, nor for all at the same time. The graces of one are not the graces of another, and "in the house of the Father there are many mansions."

When He achieves a notable success, or works a particularly striking miracle, He attributes all glory to God, without whom man cannot add to his stature one cubit. "Seek ye first the Kingdom of God." Then He effaces Himself, or asks the beneficiary to disappear. After He has raised to life the twelve-year-old daughter of Jairus, a leader of the synagogue, Our Lord forbids the parents to tell anyone about the miracle.[7] After the healing of two blind men: "See that no man know this," He warns them.[8] The leper "He charged that he should tell no man."[9] And after the healing of the man with the withered hand and other sick persons, "He

[7] Luke viii, 56;   Mark v, 43.
[8] Matt. ix, 30.
[9] Luke v, 14: Mark i, 43: Matt. vii, 4.

charged them that they should not make him known."[10] After the multiplication of the loaves He Himself disappears to escape the ovations of the crowd.

What He Himself Practiced on the occasion of His successes He bids us do in the case of any good work: "When thou dost an alms-deed, sound not a trumpet before thee, as the hypocrites do in the synagogues and in the streets, that they may be honored by men. And when thou dost alms let not thy left hand know what thy right hand doth. That thy alms may be in secret; and thy Father who seeth in secret will repay thee."[11] "And when ye pray, ye shall not be as the hypocrites that love to stand and pray in the synagogues and corners of the streets, that they may be seen by men . . . But thou when thou shalt pray, enter to thy Father in secret."[12] "When thou fastest, anoint thy head and wash thy face, that thou appear not to men to fast, but to thy Father who is in secret."[13]

Two precious lessons, therefore, from which we may derive singular profit: on the one hand a wise and patient application to

[10] Matt. vii, 16.
[11] Matt. vi, 2-4.
[12] Matt. vi, 5-6.
[13] Matt. vi, 17-18.

detail, sedulous attention to humble but important realities, and a careful choice of the best method of approach to individual souls—and on the other hand, when our efforts are crowned with success, a desire to remain hidden, and a horror of bluff and ostentation.

CHAPTER III

"...de coelis."

FROM HEAVEN

WHAT is it that we want to communicate to our brethren? Something human? No. Something divine.

And how are we to do this unless we are already, as far as possible, reservoirs of divine force? The A B C of all supernatural work is that every apostle must be an instrument united to God, *instrumentum Deo conjunctum.*

The talents and intelligence that bring success, the psychological insight that ensures delicacy and tact, the vivacity that attracts, the fine assurance that knows no timidity, the power of initiative, and the rest—all these may carry conviction. But if they are not supported by an immense reserve of divine force, the apostolate will soon stop short. You may labor much; but you will achieve nothing. There will be plenty of outward fuss; but no serious work will be accomplished. It will be a human scaffolding, to collapse with the first breath of wind.

• • • • •

The first—and obligatory—means of union with God, essential union with God, is the state of grace.

What would happen if you passed milk through a coal-sack? How much whiteness would remain after the experiment? The more pronounced the personal imperfections of an apostle are—selfishness, egoism, the spirit of criticism, pride, impurity—the more the graces of God will be adulterated, spoiled and attenuated as he attempts to transmit them to others.

From this point of view the apostolate of the laity calls for greater sanctity than that of a priest. Admittedly, by reason of the unparralleled dignity which he has received the priest is bound to strive after the highest possible degree of holiness. But his sanctity does not affect the *opus operatum* when he administers the sacraments. In other words the validity of the sacrament is—by a great mercy of God—independent of the sanctity of the minister. If the minister is holy, so much the better—he will add something to the effect of the sacrament; but the validity and efficacy of the sacrament as such is not conditioned by the holiness of him that administers it.

The layman, on the other hand, being unable to administer grace through the sacraments, can make use only of the *opus operantis*, that is to say, of his own virtue and power. And if, when he is doing his apostolic work, he is lacking in the essential degree of virtue, if he is not in the state of grace, what can he give to the world save empty words, meaningless gestures? How can he create life when he himself is a corpse? A lay apostle who is not himself alive with the life of God, or at any rate striving to live that life, is a useless cog in the machinery.

"The time is past," writes Mauriac,[1] "when men could profess principles at variance with their conduct. How many there were who used to try to reconcile the love of Catholicism with the anarchy of the soul! Our salvation lies in the fact that young people have now come to understand what is required of them in the secret recesses of their hearts, if their public life is to bear fruit."

[1] *Echo de Paris,* March 4, 1934.

And this is true not only of the present day; it is true of a fruitful apostolate for all time.

•   •   •   •   •

But the state of grace is not enough. The state of grace means that the apostle is not a bad instrument. But there are many ways of being a good instrument. An instrument may serve sufficiently, and it may serve perfectly—and there are many intermediate degrees. The best workman, the best channel of the divine, is he who is nearest to God, most conformable to His will, closest to His heart.

In a moving essay, entitled "Working with God," P.L. de Grandmaison wrote:

"It is a recognized fact that pure souls radiate purity around them, inspire good thoughts and exclude bad ones. They act like a "sacrament"—minus, of course, the grace which comes *ex opere operato*, and observing all due proportion and respect. 'God is there,' you feel like saying when you approach a Stanislaus Kostka, a John Berchmans, an Aloysius of Gonzaga, a Rose of Lima, a Catherine of Siena. It is especially children and sinners (if these last are touched by God's grace) that feel this influence, because they are especially in tune—or out of tune, and regret being out of tune—with pure souls. Hence the attraction which many men and sinners feel towards devotion to Our Lady."[2]

And so we are confronted with the question: What degree of union with God must the apostle possess? And since union with God is the fruit of recollection, the effect of the spirit and life of prayer, how far must the apostle lead a life of prayer?

Our model here must be again and always Our Lord, whether it be a question of recollection and prayer before action, or of recollection and prayer during action itself.

How did Our Lord act before beginning the preaching of the Gospel? He prayed and lived a life of recollection for thirty years. What a lesson for us, who are always wanting to get there before we start, who having only the tiniest stock-in-trade, are anxious to give out what little we have as soon as we can, and thus become bankrupt!

---

[2] *Écritis spirtuels, I, Conférences;* Beauchesne, p. 20.

Now Our Lord is about to start work. He is thirty years of age; the time has come. Now we shall hear Him. No, not yet. He goes off into the desert for forty days. He wishes His words to rest upon the support of silence, and in the desert, far from all noise and contact with men, He recollects Himself. Does He need it? Not at all; but He wants to set us an example.

And how many of us are going to profit from it? We are ready to move, act, make a great fuss. But how many of us are capable of kneeling quietly at a *prie-dieu*, with lips tightly closed, leaving the world alone for awhile? How many of us can force ourselves to be in solitude with the Master for any length of time? How many of us estimate retreats and times of recollection at their true value?

Few, I fear! And that is why an apostolate is so often ineffective. Apostolic energy is not lacking; but the apostolic energy lacks preparatory recollection. Before action there has not been enough prayer. Before starting to speak to men about God there has not been enough speaking to God about God, or rather, there has not been enough listening to God, who wants to communicate Himself to the soul and to fill it.

Moses wants to move his people. He speaks to them and they will not listen. Then Moses leaves the plains, departs from the multitude. He leaves his people; not that he intends to abandon them, but because he wants to be of greater service to them. He ascends the heights of Mount Sinai, takes off his shoes and, on the lonely heights, seeks contact with God. He recollects himself, listens, prays. When he comes down from the mountain he is no longer the same Moses. In his hands he has the true words which he has to say; not the words which he himself had invented, but the words which the Lord had dictated to him. He has around his head a light which will manifest his power, a reflection of his conversation alone with God. He has seen the invisible One, as the Bible puts it, and when the Hebrews receive him they recognize beyond all doubt that God has spoken to their leader. Moses has won the day. He casts down the golden calf; and the people offer no resistance, they listen to him. Again across the desert they follow him towards the Promised Land, in spite of hunger, thirst, serpents, in spite of all.

It was the same with the Apostle Paul. See him now, converted, burning with zeal, his mind made up to preach the Jesus whose disciples he has persecuted until now. Doubtless he will set forth without delay, going from city to city, preaching, baptizing and making converts. But no. He crosses the Jordan and takes the sandy path that leads to the heart of the Arabian desert, and there he dwells. For how long, do you think? For a few days, a few weeks? The world is waiting for him to begin his missionary journeys. Yet Paul remains in the desert for three years.

The twelve Apostles on the eve of the Ascension received command from Our Lord to preach the gospel to the world. Surely, no sooner has their Master disappeared from sight, they will set out for the four corners of the earth. Yet, see how they shut themselves up in the supper-room and remain there for nine days in prayer and recollection. "They were all persevering in prayer with Mary the Mother of Jesus." It is only after this period, when the Holy Ghost has descended upon them, that they go forth "to set the world on fire."

What a curious conception we have of the

apostolate and of the method of winning souls! How different from the methods of Jesus, of Moses, of Paul the Apostle! And yet we are surprised to find that our apostolate bears no fruit, that we fail to impress our contemporaries. Whose fault is it?

The most essential preliminary condition for all fruitful missionary work is silent prayer. The world does not need so much men who are active, it needs men who are ready to sacrifice their impetuosity, in order to make their activity fruitful by prayer.

"When man has nothing better to do, he thinks," says a humorist. What a pity! It is bad enough for the "man"; but the apostle of whom this can be said truly is no apostle at all. Thought, recollection, prayer, should be our first preoccupation.

If we only realized how much Our Lord wants us to be near Him so that in the quietness of prayer He may communicate to us the secret of the conversion of the world! It is a remarkable thing that while the Apostles dared only call themselves servants, Jesus calls them by the name of "friends." Peter calls himself *servus et apostolus Jesus Christi.*[3] James: *Domini Jesus*

---

[3] 2 Pet. i, 1.

servus.[4] Jesus Himself calls them: *Filioli.*
He is always anxious to have them near
Him. "He made that twelve should be with
Him."[5] And we often read in the Gospels:
"The twelve were with him." They are at
Cana, in the house of Simon the Pharisee;
they are present at the miracles, at the
preaching of Christ. They will never leave
Him for long. When Our Lord rests at the
well of Jacob they quickly return from the
town. *Discipuli abierant . . . continuo
venerunt discipuli.*[6] St. Luke represents Our
Lord as praying alone; but then he adds:
*Quum solus esset orans, erant cum illo et
discipuli.*[7] They are present at the scene of
the sellers in the temple, the blessing of the
children, at the Agony (though unhappily at
a distance), at the Ascension. Often when
He has spoken to the multitude Our Lord
turns and addresses a few words to them
alone. Thus after the promise of the
Eucharist, when many of His hearers have
left Him, refusing to believe, He says to His
disciples: "Will you also go away?" The
longest discourse Our Lord ever delivered
was that to His Apostles (only eleven now,
alas!) after the Last Supper.

---

[4] 2 Pet. i, 1.
[5] Mark iii, 14.
[65] John iv, 8, 27.
[7] Luke ix, 18.

The Master desired always to have His Apostles by His side; and the Apostles desired always to be with their Master. Of these two desires the first assuredly remains undiminished. But what of our desire to be as continually as possible close to the Master? We have as much time as we want for the distractions and occupations of this world. It would seem that for a heart-to-heart talk with God we cannot find a minute.

René Schwob says somewhere that "the present age has lost the secret of solitude." How true that is! "Our whole trouble," wrote La Bruyère, "comes of never being able to be alone. Hence gaming, dissipation, wine, women, uncharity, envy, forgetfulness of oneself and of God." We may add as another result, the ineffectiveness of our apostolate.

Renan said ironically of Clémenceau: "He is evidently not a man of prayer." What is the use of action, speaking, writing, external fuss, if what we sow is simply empty seed?

Silence, I mean that prayerful silence which Faber calls "an eighth sacrament," is the source of all fertility, the father of all words and all actions that are not vain. Supernatural expansion is the child of intense concentration, the child of prayer.

Words and activity are expenditure of energy; silence and prayer are its source. The brightness of the stars is only seen at night. . . . Happy those who believe that they are not wasting their time when they escape from the glaring publicity of the day, and dare to stand face to face with solitude. It is then that heaven appears. And how are we to speak of heaven if we have never "seen" it?

A Hindoo philosopher, Dhon Gopal Mukerji tells us in *Le Visage de mon frère* that after staying for twelve years in America in order to take diplomas and learn politics he was amazed to find all at once how spiritually poor he was: "When I stood on the platform of the Town Hall in New York and looked upon the faces of my audience and then looked into my own heart, I discovered with consternation that I was a man without a message. And I heard within me this clear call: 'Go back to India, and renew your spirit at the feet of Holiness.' "[8]

[8] One day the conversation turned upon Wilson, the President of the United States: "Is he a saint," he asked, "this man of the fourteen points? Has he fasted and prayed to God long enough to give each of his points an immortal life."—"No, sir; he has not fasted or prayed for fourteen years." His face cleared: "Then how can a man hope to engraft an idea upon human life without having first sacrificed many years to it?"

Of what use is it to talk and to expend energy if, having no message, I only talk to say nothing?

I have read that officers who were prisoners in Siberia during the Great War invented various devices to while away the long weary hours. One had made a drawing of a piano, another of the keys of a typewriter, a third of a Morse transmitter. And during the times of extreme boredom the pianist, with the air of one inspired, would amuse himself by passing his fingers over the mute keys, keeping time with movements of his head, correcting himself when he had struck an imaginary false note; on his blind typewriter the typist would write invisible demands upon nonexistent paper; the imaginary telegraphist sent fantastic messages, the "shorts" and the "longs" having no existence save in his dreams.

What these prisoners did out of boredom and for a psychological reason which is justifiable, I often do, perhaps for want of thought or a pure enough intention. I act, I hurry and scurry with head, arms, legs and tongue, but in the end what results do I obtain? Am I working really for God? Is it not sometimes simply the outcome of a naturally energetic temperament, and is not my motive sometimes purely human? What a pity that I should have finally to acknowledge that I have merely been "beating the air!" Perhaps I have been only touching dead keys; nothing has been written in the book of life; my appeals have not gone home. My work has been void, fruitless.[9]

A nun of the community of Saint Joseph at Cluny tells how, when traveling with Gandhi on the *Rajputana*, she and all the other travelers were struck by the recollection and the taste for prayer which the great Indian agitator manifested. Often he would go to the stern of the ship and there, his eyes closed or raised to heaven, he

---

[9] A good example of talking when you have nothing to say is to be found in this anecdote told by Wladimir d'Ormesson: When the Danish court went to the theatre, it was required that the princess and princesses should appear during the intervals to hold a very animated conversation. In order to satisfy the public, they had hit upon the idea of counting up to a hundred. "One, two, three, four, five, six," said the Prince. "Seven, eight, nine, ten, eleven," replied the Princess Royal. "Twelve, thirteen, fourteen," interrupted the Princess Ingebord, violently. "Fifteen, sixteen, seventeen, eighteen, nineteen . . ." retorted Princess Thura. "How bright and gay our princess and princesses are this evening!" thought the delighted public. (*Enfances diplomatiques, p. 27.*)

would remain absorbed in deep contemplation. "Prayer," he explained to one who
questioned him, "has been my moral and
physical salvation when in the greatest dif-
ficulties. I throw myself into the arms of
God. Then my soul has been filled with
unutterable peace even in the midst of the
greatest contradictions. Today whether I
am free or in captivity, at my ease or in
poverty, obeyed or rejected, exalted or
mocked. I am the happiest of beings; I
believe in God and trust myself to him. The
stronger my faith becomes the more I feel
the need to pray to Him. . . . Intense prayer
alone has been able to satisfy my longing for
God, and I believe that a soul can never
have too much prayer."

What a lesson for us, Catholic apostles!

And now take the case of these young
Israelites, who also understand the necessi-
ty of founding their work of apostolate on
prayer. In 1927, "Jewish Jerusalem" had
organized a "Week," a sort of retreat taking
the form of a camp, with conferences,
prayers, silent retirement. And they would
have carried their plan into execution if,
strange to relate, the Rabbis had not objected on the plea that the Israelite religion is a

community religion and does not lend itself to these individualistic manifestations of worship.[10]

We Catholics need not fear such prohibitions. Georges Duhamel calls for the foundation of a *National Park of Silence*. It is not necessary. There is an abundance of places where one can find peace and recollection. Are there not many houses of retreat? Let us profit by them. If we cannot in a particular case go to one of these places to find peace for our souls, then let us manage somehow to find a silent corner, even in the midst of turmoil. "There is always plenty of solitude for those that are worthy of it," wrote Psichari.

Take the example of these students of the Ecole d'Arts et Métiers de l'Etat, who every morning get up before the official hour of rising and meet for prayer in common. One of them writes: "The great difficulty is to cultivate the interior life. In the evening you have only the last few minutes before going to sleep. In the morning, you have to hurry to get down a few moments before the bell rings, and go out into the courtyard, to

---

[10] Bonsirven; *Sur les ruines du temple,* p. 366, Grasset (Translation published by B. O. & W.).

be able to think for a few moments and offer the day to God." He adds: "An intense interior life is absolutely necessary for any truly apostolic activity."

Other students write in a similar strain: "Several find it very hard and acknowledge it humbly. This only proves that the work of redemption cannot be carried out without great supernatural means. The more I think of it the more I am convinced that we ought all to have a more than ordinary interior life."

And another, who is already in business, writes: "I try to put more silence into and prayer into my life. On Sundays and on the days that I am traveling I give a little more time to meditation and reading. But during the week my whole day is taken up with my work. I can only be sure of a little peace in the evening, before the Blessed Sacrament in church. This is the most useful quarter of an hour in the day. It is that which gives me strength."

And here is a fine example from two statement, King Albert I of Belgium and Dollfuss, Chancellor of Austria.

When King Albert set out at the driving

wheel of his car, accompanied by his valet, Theophile van Dyck, he stopped his car a few paces from the Place du Congres.

"Wait a moment," he said simply.

Dressed in his Alpine costume he remained for ten minutes in prayer before the Blessed Sacrament. He was making his meditation. An hour later the King was dead, and that night his dead body was brought along by that same road on a gun-carriage. Many facts have been quoted in praise of the great monarch; but we know of few so much to his credit as his habit of meditation.

And when Dollfuss was asked by the President of the Austrian Republic if he would accept the post of Chancellor, the courageous leader replied: "I will give you my answer tomorrow." He made his way alone to a little church in a popular quarter of the city, where the Blessed Sacrament was exposed, and knelt down. In this decisive hour it was God's advice that this fervent Christian meant to ask. Only God's.

He remained deep in prayer until the next morning. Then, his mind made up, his duty clear, he went to the residence of the

President. He accepted.

• • • • •

That we should pray before acting is a rule which holds not only for important and vital decisions. It is a rule for everyday. For the apostle there should never be a single day which does not include some time set apart for recollection before God. This habit of constraining oneself to devote a particular time every day to prayer will engender the habit of spontaneous prayer. We shall pray almost at every moment, and especially when we are called upon to take some important action, especially an action that concerns our neighbour.

We often read in the Gospel that Our Lord before beginning some very important action recollects himself, raises His eyes to heaven. Again and again He goes apart into a mountain to pray.[11] Before the choosing of the twelve He goes up to a mountain and passes the night in communion with God.

What a lesson for us! Instead of rushing immediately upon the work that awaits us, let us wait awhile, recollect ourselves, puri-

---

[11] See Matt. xiv., 23; Mark vi, 46; Luke vi, 12 ix, 28.

fy our intention, raise our minds to God.

Especially when it is a question of forming and training His Apostles Our Lord betakes Himself to prayer; as if to prove to us that you cannot succeed in changing the hearts of men without first imploring the help of God. And again, in order to ensure that His Apostles will gain a hearing from the world, Our Lord prays likewise: "Not only for them do I pray, but for them also who through their word shall believe in me."[12]

The Acts of the Apostles gives us a remarkable picture of St. Stephen.[13] He was full of grace and fortitude, we are told, and full of faith and the Holy Ghost. And because he was a man of God he had power over souls: "He did great wonder and signs among the people . . . And they were not able to resist the wisdom and the spirit that spoke."[14]

In A. de Chateaubriant's book, *La Réponse du Seigneur,* there is a student who vaunts the superiority of action. The hero., M. de Mauvert, replies:

"Anything that leads a man away from contemplation leads him away from the true path of power. The saints, Bruno,

[12] John xviii, 20.   [13] vi, 8.   [14] vi, 8, 10.

Bernard, Benedict, found in constant contemplation the secret of their phenomenal spiritual advancement."

"After all," continues M. de Mauvert, "what is the origin of all action, and what renders it possible, if not the idea of action itself? What is action but the projection of an ideal? And have there been any great men of action who have not also been great contemplatives?"

"But that is to create a void in myself. And if I create a void in myself, what is left?"

"In the void that you make, await Him who is."

When a soul possess God, that is, when a soul is in a state of grace, when it is also "possessed" by God, that is, when it strives as often as possible to come into contact with God (the state of habitual recollection)—then it can approach others. It may not be evident, even to the soul itself. that it is imparting divine powers to others; Our Lord may sometimes permit that nothing is imparted to others. But in fact, through that soul God will have found a way into certain other souls, and to others He will have revealed Himself more clearly.

He who possesses God, and possesses Him in heart that is free from encumbrances, he who possesses God in that void of which the author just quoted speaks, the void that excludes useless nothings to make place for the only true and substantial Reality, such a one cannot fail to have great influence upon his fellows.

The more you feel the desire to give much, the more frequently should you have recourse to the source of all. Referring to Our Lord, Pascal writes: "The artisan who talks about riches, the solicitor who talks about war, soon betrays his ignorance and gives himself away. But the rich man talks well about riches . . . that is to say, God talks well about God." If the language of Our Lord is a proof of the divinity of His Person, the language of an apostle shows whether or not he is a man of God. If he is simply a man, and nothing more, then he will do better to hold his tongue.

BOOK II

"Incarnatus est."

INCARNATION

CHAPTER I

MAKING THE TRUTH VISIBLE

THE descent from heaven is only the first stage in the conquest of souls. To save us God willed to become incarnate. After His example, and in a manner later to be determined, every apostle must endeavour to do the same.

What does this mean?

It means that the apostle in his own person must, first, make the truth visible; and this will be the subject of the present chapter. Secondly, he must make the truth lovable by presenting it as attractively as he can. Thirdly, he must make the truth admirable by becoming, as far as possible, an heroic example of Christian virtue. The latter two points will be explained in the following chapters. To help us to achieve our destiny, God was not content merely to give us a conscience which should guide us according to the law of reason; he completed the natural law by a positive teaching: Revelation. But what use is a word which is nothing more than a word, were it even a divine word? Man always feels the need of seeing, touching, feeling; and he does not allow himself to be easily won by a divine Word which is a word and nothing more. Through the whole of the Old Testament we see how God endeavored to keep man in the path of duty by recalling to him the require- ments of the Word. But what does Jeru- salem do? She pays no heed; and what is worse, she kills those who are sent to her, she stones the prophets.

And so the Word becomes incarnate. The Message, instead of remaining a mere mes- sage, becomes a living life amongst us. The Word becomes flesh. And the Gospel is more than a lesson, much more; it is an example.

A word by itself has rarely any motive power, is rarely dynamic. Let an officer show his men the written order received from his superior, that they are to "go over the top," to go and meet death. They are so many words on paper, and the men will not budge. But let him advance at the head of his company; then the men will follow him.

You will not carry men away by talking to them; but you will, if you let them see. When the philosopher lays down as a moral axiom: "So act that your manner of action may become a universal rule," the majority of men are not convinced. Universal rule? Who cares for that? The great advantage of the religion of Jesus our Saviour is that it is not merely a form of belief to be accepted, it shows this formula alive in a being of flesh and blood. You may follow Aristotle without knowing anything about Aristotle; you may follow Plato or Kant without knowing anything about Plato or Kant. It is not a matter of their person, it is a matter of their teaching. The Gospel is not merely a manifestation of the teaching of Christ, it is the manifestation of His Person.

To believe does not mean only adherence to a dead text, it means submission to a living Person. So St. John writes in his first Epistle[1]: "That which was from the beginning, which we have heard, which we have seen with our eyes, which we have looked upon and our hands have handled, of the Word of life . . . that which we have seen and have heard, we declare unto you." "The Life," he says, "was manifested." And in the prologue of his Gospel, having written: "The Word was made flesh," he adds: "We have seen his glory." *Et vidimus.*

[1] i, 1-3.

"You can only govern man by the imagination," said Bonaparte, and that is the reason why always, in order to make a doctrine dynamic, men have sought to embody it, to make it incarnate, to give it a body. The revolutionaries of 1793 set up in the church of Notre-Dame a goddess Reason of flesh and blood; they embodied the suppression of ancient abuses in the Capture of the Bastille. If a man has been a good citizen, men will set up beside his bust statues representing the civic virtues; if a poet, a woman as the symbol of inspiration.

It is a universal rule. Abstract language will move no one. Embody it in a well devised image and it will live. An abstract formula leaves men cold; give it a body and it begins to act.[2]

This is especially true of a rule of life. An ethical formula counts for little; example is everything. If Christ had called us to the practice of poverty solely by His teaching in

---

[2] So true is this, that sometimes a word or a gesture, or both together, will prove effective, even when the idea is non-existent or not understood. Thus a wild beast obeys the eye of his tamer, an audience obeys the pantomime of an orator, the sound of his voice; they are carried away sometimes even when they disapprove of his views.

the sermon on the Mount: "Blessed are the poor," then few men would have sought blessedness in poverty. Christ lived a poor man; He was born poor, He died poor; it was more by His example than by His word that He drew Francis of Assisi and Foucauld— and a legion of others more or less like them—to follow Him.

To talk is a good thing. But to act is very much better. Of Him, Our Lord, it could be said: *Coepit facere et docere.* He did and he taught; but notice, He began by doing. His whole life is summed up in the words: *Bene omnia fecit.* He did all things well. Even His enemies have no fault to find with Him. *Non invenio in eo causam;* "I find no cause in Him," said Pilate. Nothing in Him is worthy of blame. All is perfection.

In the rites that He instituted, Our Lord connected the granting of grace with a visible thing; the sacraments. Always the same principle of Incarnation. And if the Church after the example of Our Lord recommends prayer in silence and solitude, she also preaches external cult, the use of images and the visible manifestations of the Liturgy.

• • • • •

The apostle, then, will strive to acquire the maximum of human and supernatural qualities. Human qualities are by no means the most important, admittedly. But they have—some of them at least—a power of attraction which certain of the virtues do not possess.

The apostle must be as much a *man* as possible. Our Lord was a man in the fullest and most magnificent sense of the word. Responsive to all the beauties of nature, He loves the wayside flower and the golden moss, the vine and the fig tree, the bright light of the heavens and the majesty of the temple. Responsive to all His brethren, He is with them in their sorrows and their joys: He sheds tears over Lazarus, over Jerusalem, over the son of the widow of Naim, over the little daughter of the officer Jairus, and He joins amicably in the festivities of Cana and of Simon the Pharisee. He is not pontifical or sententious, always He shows Himself cordial, simple, approachable. His chief quality is His good-nature, "a smiling self-abandonment." He knows all things, but He overwhelms none with His learning; at the age of twelve He talks easily with the doctors of Israel; He amazes them *(mirabantur omnes)*, but He gives no offence. His disciples, the multitude, even His judges, have to admit that in matters of divine knowledge He is an edept without equal. This is self-evident, but He does not strive to make it evident. And side by side with that simplicity which is so attractive, there is a majesty so gentle, an air of greatness so modest, a nobility of manner so spontaneous. *Curialissimus homo*, one of the Fathers called Him later. "A great gentleman," indeed; but there is nothing about Him of the "tower of ivory"; the portcullis is always down and anyone may always enter freely. "Suffer them to come to me," and the little ones, who are always at their ease with the truly great, know Him by instinct. His arms are always open.

Like Christ, the apostle must be a man in the widest possible sense: able to understand all, to love all, to appreciate all; he must have "feelers," he must possess the gift of sympathy, and he must acquire the highest possible degree of competence. Yet withal he must be ever modest. We have spoken of humility, and how necessary it is if we are to attract people. An air of superiority, a show of greatness, always offends. Let your merit appear, but do not make a show of it. True nobility of character is always humble; great men of learning, great artists, great politicians, great soldiers, in general, are modest; if they are not, something is lacking to their greatness, to their attractiveness.

Open-heartedness, competence, good-nature, nobility of character and demeanour, all these united with an easy and affable manner—such are the qualities which for being natural are none the less most valu-able in an apostle, especially in the young.

• • • • •

If it is important to present a humanity richly endowed with human gifts, it is above all necessary that through our humanity we should show forth Christ, and manifest the beauty of life as lived according to the Gospel. Perrèyve used to pray: "Jesus when they see me may they recognize Thee." Exactly.

A young apprentice, who had been work-ing only for a short time in a factory, was asked by a priest:

"Do your fellow-workers know the Gospel?"

"No, they do not know the Gospel."

"Do they know Jesus Christ?"

"No, they do not know Jesus Christ."

"Or the Pope?"

"No."

"Or the Bishop?"

"No."

"Or M. le Curé?"

"No."

"Then listen; you are going to have the honour of making all these things known to your fellow-workers. When they see you, they must learn something about this Christianity of which they know nothing. It is for you to radiate the Gospel. When they see you, let them discover Jesus Christ!"

This is the essential mission of the apostle; to be a living witness to the greatness and beauty of Christianity; especially at the present day, when so many people have concerning religion only false ideas, prejudices, or total lack of understanding.

We are "messengers of light," as Claudel

put it. He was writing to Jacques Rivière:
"You have the leisure, you have the intelligence, you are the messenger of light for
these unfortunate souls. What will you
answer when they accuse you before God,
and ask: 'What have you done with these
talents?' "

We have not all the same leisure, the
same intelligence, the same degree of
instruction, but all of us, according to the
gifts we have received, are bound to make
the truth known by letting it shine forth in
us. "You," asks Claudel again, this time
addressing all Christians, "who have the
light, what are you doing with it?"

May we not all make our own the prayer
of Katherine Mansfield: "Lord, make me
like crystal so that thy light may shine
through me" Light penetrates everywhere,
and in penetrating is not soiled. It is the
work of the apostle to penetrate all sorts of
surroundings, bringing with him the truth
and love of Jesus Christ; and he must be
able to go anywhere with impunity.

"I pray not," says Our Lord, speaking of
His disciples, "that thou shouldst take them
out of the world, but that thou shouldst
deliver them from evil." It is so easy to let

oneself be influenced by one's surroundings, to be crushed by the mass instead of penetrating it like leaven.

Berdiaeff writes[3]: "The Socialists assert that throughout the history of human society a privileged minority has fattened upon the unfortunate majority. But there is another and a deeper truth which is less apparent at first sight. It is that the masses, that is the quantitative majority, have throughout history oppressed and persecuted the qualitative minority, those individual minds that are turned towards the heights of the sublime. History has evolved in favour of the average man, the masses; it is for them that the State was created, the family, juridicial institutions, the school, the whole code of manners and customs. . . . It is the average man, the man of the masses, that has always dominated history, always demanded that everything should be done for him, for his interests and on his level."

The great danger of "the world," in the sense in which Our Lord speaks of the world is that of dragging things down to the level of the average, that of spreading the

[3] *Esprit et Liberté,* pp. 16-17. (Ed. *Je sers,* 1933.)

slow poison of mediocrity. It is not directly the instigation to sin; it is the fascination of all that makes one weak in the face of sin; it dethrones the ideal, scorns enthusiasms, tends to reduce everything to the level of the commonplace. It is the death of the "Excelsior" spirit. It glories in omissions; its danger lies less in what it demands than in what it obstructs.

The man who lets himself be influenced by such an atmosphere is lost for all generous effort, he will never be one of the elite. Nominally he may remain upon the list of workers, but it will be risky to make use of him. Not strong enough to resist, not fully enough convinced to react against the fascination of error, he is acted upon by others instead of acting upon them; instead of leading the flock, it is the flock that leads him. Communion with the less good has made him less good; he has become "so-so"—one of the crowd. Is he leaven for the masses? On the contrary, he is part of the mass that needs to be leavened.

Our Lord did not come for the sake of those who are well, but for those who are in need; the soul that is lost interests Him far more than the ninety-nine that are just, the venturesome lamb that has fallen into the pit far more than the flock that has returned dutifully home; the coin that has rolled behind the furniture, far more than the fortune in the cash-box. His interest is in the prodigals: Magdalene, the woman taken in adultery, Zacheus the publican, Simon the Pharisee, Barabbas, and his companion on the cross.

The preferences of the apostle should be of the same kind. But what integrity this demands, what moral beauty, what sanctity!

•　•　•　•　•

Some perhaps may be tempted to escape the corrosive or weakening effect of such surroundings by avoiding to much contact with the masses, by seeking the company of their friends especially, of those who think alike with them, and to whom they feel more readily attracted. It is so much more pleasant to consort with those who are like yourself, with whom you have ideals and interests in common.

Such a method is disastrous. If the leaven is to act upon the mass it must be mingled with it; if it is separate from the mass it forgets its proper task. It is a leading axiom in Catholic Action not to remove good elements from the surroundings in which they exist, but rather so to sanctify them that they may serve to elevate and improve their fellows.

Vigny—wrongly, by the way—makes Moses exclaim: "Alas, Lord, thou hast made me wise among the wise. Alas, Lord, I am powerful and alone."

It is good to be wise among the wise; it is good to be powerful, too. But alone, no! To act effectively upon one's surroundings, one must live in those surroundings; and given the necessary virtue and power of action, the closer the contact the greater the influence will be.

CHAPTER II

MAKING THE TRUTH LOVABLE

THE Gospel has its austere side. As Pascal says, if it were nothing but geometry few would refuse to accept it. That there are three persons in one God is not the truth that worries most people. The Gospel contains a moral code, it demands a manner of acting and a behaviour in which nature sees nothing but restraints, and therefore nature fears it. And this is especially true of the young. At an age when senses, desire and curiosity are beginning to awake, any prospect of restraint is repellent.

It is a mistake, especially with the young, to present the religion of Our Savior Jesus Christ from the purely *negative* side: what is forbidden, what must not be done. Christianity thus appears as a barrier-religion, a religion which makes for the attenuation of being and life, whereas the Gospel is essentially and chiefly quite the opposite.

The doctrine of Our Saviour offers a magnificent vista of expansion. The Son of God did not come on earth to bind us hand and foot, to impose various police regulations more or less of an unreasonable character. If He became man it was in order to bring us something unique, something absolutely extraordinary.

Bergson concludes *Les Deux Sources* with an incisive sentence. He calls upon the human race "to make the effort necessary to accomplish upon our refractory planet the essential function of the universe, which is a machine for the making of gods."

His words are more true than he imagines. Is it not literally true that of us it has been said *Dii estis;* "ye are gods," and that we are to become "sons of God"? Let us give to these expressions there fullness of Christian meaning.

First and foremost, then, the baptized must learn to appreciate the incomparable privileges they have received by that sacrament which, in making them Christians, has brought the Blessed Trinity to dwell in their souls, and govern them power to live the divine life, if only they will, and so long as they will. Let us lift up our heads; let us bear proudly the proud dignity of our baptism.

In the days when it was not the custom to go about the streets with head uncovered, there was at Montmarte a good old man, of whom Léon Bloy tells us that he went about in all weathers carrying his hat in his hand. Why? Because he was always walking in the presence of God, and therefore he always went with head uncovered. An eccentricity, if you will; but a fine act of faith.

How few of the baptized appreciate this sublimes of all revelations: that God dwells in the man who is in the state of grace? This is the campaign that is most urgently needed: to help each and everyone to realize fully, perhaps for the first time, the divine dignity that Baptism confers by engrafting us upon Christ himself, making us a living member of the mystical body of Christ, which is the Church, communicating to us the very life of the Blessed Trinity, making us partners in the royal priesthood of Christ and His Church, uniting us in a common kinship with all our baptized brethren by this spiritual solidarity which is the communion of saints, consecrating us as living chalices, as living temples to the personal and social worship of the true God.

Does not this discovery fill us with enthusiasm? Let us beware in our spiritual lives of concentrating exclusively upon sin. Sin becomes an obsession: One sees it everywhere, its power and its fascination are exaggerated; you would almost think that the power of satan is equal to that of God, the power of Anti-Christ equal to that of Christ. Why give sin this halo, why make it loom so large that it blocks all else out of sight. Sin exists, of course. It would be foolish to deny it. But it exists in its own place, and that is not the first place. The first thing I have to do is, not to avoid sin, but to live the divine life. First comes the splendour of the state of grace; sin, wickedness, fills us with horror. True spiritual hygiene consists not in being hypnotized by the world of evil, but in concentrating upon the good, upon the world of God, upon the vision of light.

"It is not by the repugnance of ugliness," writes Péguy, "that we must teach beauty, but by the attractiveness of beauty itself." He is right. Are we or are we not, sons of a King? Are we, or are we not, sons of God? Are we, or are we not, living tabernacles of the Blessed Trinity? Are we, or are we not, living prolongations of Christ? That is what counts, this is more important than anything else.

That in consequence of this baptismal glory we must always in all circumstances behave as a baptized person should behave, as behaves a living tabernacle of the Blessed Trinity, a child of the Redemption, one who is truly consecrated, of this there can be no doubt. And if the fulfillment of this royal programme, if the task of making our work, our gestures, our words, thoughts and feelings worthy of a baptized person entails sacrificing some indulgence, some visit, a half-a-pint of beer, a cinema, then let us be glad to make the sacrifice. Restriction? Not at all. We are the richer thereby. To transform the shapeless block of marble into the radiant statue of his dreams the sculptor strikes and chips the marble. To spoil his marble? No, to give it a new beauty.

It is one of the most subtle temptations of the Evil One to persuade you that self-conquest means self-weakening, that to train oneself means to enfeeble one's energies. Renan once said, in his skeptical and apparently detached manner: "Truth is perhaps an unpleasant thing." Claudel, writing to

Jacques Rivière, rightly stigmatizes "the detestable words of this hideous Renan," and tells how they revolted him even before his conversion. "Already in my heart I knew that the only true reality is joy in God, and that the man who knows it not will never do the work of an artist as he will never do the work of a saint."

Gide does not even retain the "perhaps" of the statement of Renan. For him it is a dogma. Having for a long time resisted the sting of the flesh he succumbed in the end, and—as the weak are wont to do—he tried to give an explanation of his fall. To fall, he says, is to become enriched. We should taste every joy, strike every note of the keyboard, drink at every source. No distinction is to be made between forbidden joys and healthy joys; all is good, all is healthy. You can never have too wide an experience. All honour to the man that has experienced everything, even the worst.

As if it did no harm to mix poison with pure flour! Truly it must take a massive credulity to accept such a sophistry.

Evil does not enrich. Sin has no beauty; it fascinates man, it is true; but in itself it is not fascinating. Man is attracted by a mirage. The devil is not amusing. He can amuse; which is something quite different. Not that he has in himself a power of attraction, but because there is in us a power of misunderstanding and illusion; because we remain content with appearances and do not go to the heart of reality. Evil is non-being, evil is a void. It may wear a mask, but that is what it is essentially. And therefore instead of developing our powers it attenuates them; instead of giving true joy it yields boredom. And that is proved evidently by the experience of those who have reached a certain limit in evil. That taste of ashes in the mouth, that rancour, that emptiness—that is the true taste of sin. Evil is an unpleasant thing.

Away, then, with the theories of renan and Gide; they are specious but false. Evil is evil, not because it is forbidden but because it is non-being; essentially it is a privation; and to gratify one's appetites with a privation is not to become enriched. You might as well say that dry bread is equivalent to a good dinner.

We must oppose that custom whereby virtue is dissociated from the idea of happiness, and "joy" always associated with sin.

It is sin that brings unhappiness. Virtue, whatever sacrifices it may entail, is really and truly that which gives joy.

It was Ernest Psichari, the grandson of Renan, who said when he was definitely on the way to conversion: "I knew where I was going. I was going towards the abode of peace, I was going to joy. I wept with love, happiness and gratitude." Claudel wrote in a like strain to Jacques Rivière: "Whatever you may think, you will never approach happiness without approaching its source which is God and Christ."

There you have the truth: approaching true joy means drawing near to God; to draw near to God is to draw near to true happiness.

• • • • •

After the example of Christ, therefore, we must not present Christian doctrine, especially to the young, under an exclusively negative form. But that is not all: we must strive always to present it under its most attractive aspect.

Let us watch Our Lord. How does He proceed?

He is preaching His sermon on the Mount. He wishes to give to the world His great lessons of detachment, purity and charity, and He knows well that these may easily cause the timid to shrink and even the willing to hesitate. Accordingly He avoids making a series of demands; he gives a recipe for happiness.

Would you be happy? Then act thus and thus. He puts in the foreground not His rights but our happiness. *Beati, beati.* A recipe for happiness must surely be greeted with smiles. That would be worthy buying; anyone would pay a price for that.

Even when Our Lord is speaking directly of the Cross and of the duty of practising needful self-denial, He is careful to add the motive which allures: "If any man would come after me." The service of God is presented as a friendship before it appears as a renunciation. A renunciation is repugnant, but a friendship attracts; and history shows that this friendship has appeared so attractive that multitudes of souls have chosen to follow Our Lord even to the length of giving up all, even to the most perfect imitation, even to the folly of the cross.

Let us use the same method in our apos-

tolate. Not that we are to use deceit in order
to hide what Christian doctrine demands of
us; but we should begin by pointing out the
rich potentialities of development that
Christian doctrine contains. Nobody is such
a fool as to think that diamonds can be
bought for a few pence. And none will think
that the precious pearl can be found without paying a price. The important thing is to
show the value of the pearl, to present it in
favourable light. Arouse enthusiasm. Sacrifice will follow.

CHAPTER III

MAKING THE TRUTH ADMIRABLE

To present Christian doctrine in all its positive richness, and even where it demands sacrifices to insist upon the fulness of life which such sacrifices develop, is already a method which will bear much fruit. But we must do more.

We have to make Christian teaching attractive by presenting it in action, by furnishing an example of Christian life which will be not only attractive, but, if possible, even heroic. We have to make the truth admirable.

Words may be effective; but actions have a hundred times there value in power of persuasion. And among actions the most persuasive of all are those which are marked with the stamp of heroism. That is why St. John the Baptist won so many disciples. He was, as the Gospel says, "a burning and a shining light," and for that reason many were "willing to rejoice in his light." With Our Lord it was the same. He attract-

ed more by His example than by His words;
and if He attracted men more than did St.
John the Baptist, it was because the example which He gave to the world and the wonders which He worked far surpassed those
of the Precursor. "I have a greater testimony than that of John; for the works which
the Father hath given me to perfect, the
works themselves which I do, give testimony of me that the Father hath sent me."[1]

And the works which the Father gave
Him to perfect were not only His miracles;
there was also the astounding sanctity of
His life. Heroic in poverty and detachment;
heroic in His courage before the Pharisees
and before His judges; heroic in accepting
suffering; heroic in His love for men.

Why is the example of Christ so alluring?
Not merely beause it is an example, but
because it is an example of such extreme
devotednesss that it compels admiration
and, in those who fully appreciate it, engen-
ders an immeasurable love.

To appreciate the poverty of Our lord it is
enough to look at the manger. Joseph and
Mary were poor, but at least they had their
home at Nazareth. Yet they must leave

[1] John v, 36.

their home, and Jesus is born by the road-side in a cattle-shed. Surely He will be allowed to pass the early years of His infancy in the home of His parents. No. There is Herod, the persecution, the massacre of the Innocents; He must flee into Egypt. Later during His public life He depends upon the chance hospitality accorded Him; He has not a stone whereon to lay His head.

And His courage in facing the Pharisees and His judges! When the sellers desecrate the temple He does not hesitate to take the scourge in hand against them. He lays bare the malice of the faithless and hypocritical Pharisees, and when they rave about the empty observance of the law, He shows how vain is a worship which has no soul. Envy and hatred pursue Him in consequence. But of that He takes no heed. Before His judges He knows that if He states the truth openly it will cost Him His life. Not for a moment does He hesitate.

And with what calm tranquility He accepts suffering! He knows what the salvation of the world will cost Him: *oblatus est quia ipse vuluit*. He was offered because He willed it. He must die by a cruel crucifixion: *crucifixus eltiam pro nobis*. And the motive of His sacrifice is His love for fallen humanity, for a humanity shorn of all its divine perfections. He who loves gives up his life. Greater love no man hath: *in finem dilexit.*

• • • • •

The more capable an apostle is of presenting an heroic embodiment of virtue, the better apostle will he be. Men surrender to whatever surpasses the ordinary. We need something far more than ordinary virtue. Average people as a rule achieve little; to attract the masses and carry them with you, you must stand above the common level. St. Ignatius required of his companions that they should be "outstanding" in the service of God; he demanded something far more than a half-hearted service, more than "carpet-slipper" loyalty.

Every apostle must aim at being an outstanding apostle; he must strive to reproduce in himself the qualities of his Master; outstanding detachment, outstanding boldness, outstanding spirit of sacrifice, outstanding charity.

It would be impossible in these days to exaggerate the importance of detachment from the comforts of life, if any influence is to be exerted upon one's fellows. Our age is an age of frenzied love of pleasure; the mass, the herd, only wants self-indulgence. They say: between the past war, during which we were too much restricted, and the conflagrations to come, during which we shall have perforce to be restricted again, let us open the sluices and let ourselves go: every pleasure, every satisfaction, the body, the flesh, nudism in theory and in practice, erotic publications flourishing, attacks on the marriage laws, the quest of artificial and sophisticated pleasures, casinos, gaming-dens, cinemas, gambling and jobbery, anything, so long as you have money to buy it.

We need a Francis of Assisi. More then ever today, the world needs to learn contempt for all that is transitory, for the false glitter of worldly joys, and to follow only one Master, Christ.

There was Foucauld, but he set up his tent in Africa; he should have set it up in the over-populated but empty desert of our cities of Europe. The Sahara is too far away. We need an example in the midst of Paris.

There are some young people who have shown that they understand the meaning of true values; they are not afraid to publish their contempt for soft living. For several weeks every year they set off. No soft beds for them; they prefer the hard ground. No delicate foods either; just what an improvised kitchen can manage to produce; and instead of the sham decorations of our theatres and pleasure resorts, the open air, God's sun, the joy of the freshening wind, climbing the heights, singing a song in spite of the rain, the dust or the heat. Down with artificial pleasures! For them, the open air.

Open air for the body. But especially for the soul. The task before the apostle is to re-create the code of Christianity in a pagan world, and that is a task that calls for heroes. To give life to the inert, to bury the corpses, to arouse enthusiasm, to force the mass to receive the leaven and react to it, all this needs something more than emasculated Christians:

"I realize the immense work that we have to do in ourselves before we can make any impression. The masses are gross, bestial, though there are some fine characters. Above all there is much of the herd instinct, and the quest of pleasure. You need to be strong to make any impression there, and the ordinary good fellow is not the man to succeed. People will have nothing to do with that type. I have often noticed how much unbelievers demand of believers before they will admire or follow them. They will only submit to the influence of the strong. Anything in the nature of affectation, softness or readiness to compromise is already condemned beforehand."[2]

There is no need to be afraid of asking too much. What attracts the young especially is the hard task, the difficult exploit. If you want volunteers for easy work, they are not enthusiastic. When faced with the choice of a religious order, souls that have a vocation seem by instinct to adopt those orders which are more fervent and more exacting. Similarly souls will only enroll themselves in the service of a leader or an organization if they see that there are sacrifices to make and hard work to do.

Moreover, to-day we need charity, a greathearted charity. One cannot love too much. Francis of Assisi and Foucauld impressed the world by their poverty, but still more by their charity.

It is not so easy to love—we are speaking here of Christian love, that is, supernatural

[2] *Jean Baron:* Maritain, pp. 166, 173, 177.

love. The world can love in a human way; but we have to love in a divine way, that is, we must see in others, however little they may attract our human love, the presence of the Lord and the seal of Christ. Rank, nationality, and legitimate barriers; but beyond these we must learn to recognize what the eyes of the body cannot see and faith only can reveal. We do not understand sufficiently the Communion of Saints. At the present day it is enough to say, in certain quarters, that you love, to fall into disgrace. It is the unpardonable sin.

Admittedly, there are different ways of loving, and we are not advocating that form of humanitarianism which has no consistency or laws, and has nothing in common with the charity of Christ.

Before talking of love as between class and class, and nation and nation, may we not well ask ourselves what sort of love we bear towards our fellow-workers or our brethren in the social circle in which we live our daily lives? One of the best of the books of the day is entitled: "If only we knew how to love." Alas! We do not.

BOOK III

". . . passus.

SUFFERING

CHAPTER I

SACRIFICE AND SANCTITY

To stoop to souls as the Son of God did, to adapt oneself to them, to put oneself on their level and within their reach; and to do this not as one who comes from the same region as they, but as one that comes from the serene heights of prayer, from heaven, from God—*descendit de coelis;* and secondly, to become incarnate, to take visible shape, to transform words into example, and if possible into so transcending an example as to attract the souls of others—*incarnatus est.* All this is much. But it is not yet enough.

He who would exercise his power of redeeming to the utmost limit, as Christ did, must not shrink from that which awaits all saviours: the cross—*passus, crucifixus est.* Souls are won by words, they are won by example; but above all they are won by sacrifice. "When I am weak," wrote St. Paul, "then I am strong." In this conflict it is those that fall who are victorious; the salvation of the world belongs to the crucified.

Suffering means, in the first place, to embrace the sacrifice which is necessary in order to destroy anything in oneself that may obstruct the work of Redemption. A negative task, but an essential and indispensable one.

It costs a lot to make a Christian, a true Christian. To be perfect as our heavenly Father is perfect is no small thing. And I may not aspire to anything less. I must not rest until "Christ is formed in me," as St. Paul and the Gospel require. My vocation as a Christian means that I must become "another Christ," a living continuation of Jesus our Saviour; to that I am called by my baptism. But to this transformation into Jesus Christ, to this "transubstantiation," as one might call it, my lower nature offers a thousand obstacles. Paul said: "I live, now not I, but Christ liveth in me." But I am far from being able to say the same; the "I" is very strong in me, it lives vigorously and asks only to live an even fuller life. The slightest sacrifice costs me a lot: to do somebody a favour, to give up some food that I like, to give up a dance, or to resist excessive curiosity in looking at a passer-by, to correct untidy habits, to devote myself diligently to my work, such things for me are an affair of state.

At the consecration of the Mass the bread is an inert matter, and when the irresistible words are pronounced: "This is my body," there is nothing left of the bread; it is all instantaneously changed into Jesus Christ.

But my nature is not inert, it is a living reality. And it cannot be changed in an instant, because every particle of "me" offers resistance. It feels that it is wrong, that it ought to offer itself to so desirable a transformation; but courage is lacking. Moreover, the atmosphere that surrounds us is not propitious to renunciation. Nothing invites us to a life of detachment; and if events demand sacrifice, the majority turn a deaf ear, and only accept it with grumblings and complaints at the privations they are forced to undergo.

Statistics show that in the year 1931 the total receipts of the places of entertainment in Paris-theatres, casinos, cinemas, concerts—amounted to 709 million, or 200 francs per head of the total population, that is to say 400 or 500 francs for every adult.

That a collector should be willing to pay 100,000 francs for the MS. of a famous play may perhaps be understood. But to pay 4,583,886 francs for a ring is a little excessive, even for a music-hall artiste. If a film actor dies, the papers immediately proclaim delightedly to the world that he leaves eight motor-cars, twelve dogs, fifty pairs of socks and two thousand shirts! And I have read somewhere that in the United States women spend thirty million dollars daily on beauty products; an American woman thus spends three times more on her beauty than on her food.

These facts hardly astonish us. But those who have nothing, or whose fortune is gradually on the wane, cannot help throwing a glance of envy at people who can "amuse" themselves in this way.

Even the very thought or the reminder of sacrifice is repugnant. Not only do people not want the Cross, they do not even want to hear it talked about. The writer of these lines had written a modest work whose title recalled the Cross: a Catholic lady—in the eyes of the world an excellent Catholic-said: "Why did you give the book such a title? How will you ever get people to read it? They want something more attractive."

And that reminds me of a dialogue heard

at the Missionary Exhibition in 1931, in a chapel under which there was a crypt of the martyrs. A lady asked her husband: "What is down there?"—"The crypt of the martyrs."—"Oh no! I don't want to see anything horrible like that."

And yet in mundane affairs people do not mind making sacrifices. A woman can display immense courage and energy to save her husband from the camps of the Soviet;[1] and yet for Christ's sake it would seem that we are incapable of making the smallest renunciation!

Think of the young fellow who lost his eyes during the war, but made up his mind that it should make no difference to him. He continued to ride a bicycle and a horse; he took up the study of law, became a barrister, studied his briefs, pleaded in court; he took up politics, studied the newspapers, devoted himself to the questions of the day, became a member of the chambre des Deputés—and when interviewed was able to say; "If I have lost ninety per cent of my capacity for happiness, my capacity for work has remained the same." If he could make that generous

---

[1] Tatiana Tchernavina: *Echappés du Guépéou* (Payot).

effort merely to retain his place among men, can we not show a little energy on behalf of Christ?

Beethoven the great musician who was later to be afflicted with deafness, said: "Sacrifice all the follies of life to your art." In his diary he wrote, in the year 1796: "In spite of my bodily weakness my genius will triumph. I am twenty-five years old. This very year the whole man must reveal himself."

And our eighteen, twenty, twenty-five years? What are we going to do with them for Christ?

CHAPTER II

SACRIFICE AND CONQUEST

SACRIFICE is necessary as a preliminary condition of the apostolate: you cannot be a saviour unless you are "another Christ," and you cannot be "another Christ" unless you are, to some extent at any rate, crucified as Christ was.

But we must go further, and say: sacrifice is important as being the principal means of winning souls. And first, because of its value as an example.

Of those who do not accept the Gospel, few deny that the Gospel possesses the one true way of salvation; but what many of them seek, and seek in vain, unfortunately, is preachers of the Gospel who begin by living what they demand of others. Garric puts the matter very well when he writes:

"The world today awaits a Saint Francis of Assisi as an apostle of peace. But St. Francis had first renounced his mantle and his robe. Who among us has stripped himself?

It is not enough at the present day to "talk"—if indeed it ever was enough. We must show the world how the Gospel is "lived." Orators, speakers, are not lacking; indeed there is a glut of them. It is not so much people who are ready to mount the platform that we need, as people who are ready to mount the cross.

In a magnificent conference (the 39th, towards the end) Lacordaire, speaking of the triumph of the Gospel in the early days of Christianity, writes:

"What force had the kingdom of souls at its disposal against the empire armed with its legions? The early Christians had only the same force that Jesus Christ had. They had only to confess His name, and then die, die today, die tomorrow, die always. They had, that is, to conquer servitude by the pacific use of the freedom of the soul; they had to conquer force, not by force, but by virtue. They had been told: If for three centuries you can say aloud: I believe in God the father almighty, creator of heaven and earth, and in Jesus Christ His only Son, Our Lord, who was born of the Virgin Mary, died and rose again—if you can say all this aloud for three centuries, and die every day after having said it, then in three centuries you shall be the masters, that is, you shall be free."

P. Gatry shows that the law has remained the same for the present day: it is sacrifice that will save the world:

"A small number of intelligent and determined workers, to-day more than at any other period, could influence the course of the whole world. But even this small devoted band is not to be found. Everyone is wrapped up in his own pleasures, in his own business. People cannot, will not, change their lives and devote them to the work of saving the world. . . . Nowadays everybody is carried away by the strong tide of youth. They listen; for a moment they seem to hesitate. But the torrent of life carries them away, and they are borne off on the sterile tide of empty days. They go on thus to the end, and they have not known God, nor their soul, nor the kingdom of God; and then they die. O my God, among the immense number of those that are called how few are your chosen ones!"[1]

But we find these chosen ones sometimes. On the back of the mortuary card of Jacque Couty, a young student of Termier's at the

[1] *Comment. sur l'Evangile de Saint Matt.,* II, 163.

École des Mines, who died like a saint at the age of twenty-one, the following sentence was printed: "The most important thing in life is to be never satisfied, either with oneself or with one's portion of knowledge, and to seek always to strive and to rise."

So many people are so easily satisfied! Their hearts are not open to great things. An average personality, average happiness, average ideals are enough for them. They are content to be one of the herd.

What Our Lord demands of His Apostles is: to beware of being ordinary, to be a contrast to the masses, not through vanity but for the sake of their apostolate, and to love the cross in the midst of a world that denied the cross. "Follow me," He says, "and I will make you fishers of men." Follow Me, leave the ordinary, the commonplace, leave comfort and egoism; be willing to suffer, be willing not to be like others, to cut yourself off from everything that is not Me; only on this condition can the work of the apostle be done. Follow Me; on this condition, and on this condition alone, "I will make you fishers of men."[2] And to St. Peter in particular He said: "Henceforth thou shalt catch men,"

[2] Matt. iv, 19.

that is, when he had accepted the necessary detachment from all things on earth.

And what was the response of the Apostles? They knew what had been their Master's lot. They would have to brave fatigue—*Jesus fatigatus ex itinere;* thirst, as Jesus suffered at Jacob's well; hunger—"afterwards He was hungry." If this was the lot of their Master, could they hope for greater comfort?

And in this sense, they understood their mission. They were fond of their nets; they gave up their nets—*relictis retibus;* they were fond of their country; they left their own country—*Profecti praedicaverunt ubique.* They were like the African who, being asked by a European what was his country, answered: "My country is the whole earth." And it needs perhaps as much self-denial to opens one's heart to embrace all, as to shut one's heart in privation; to be willing to conquer the earth when one is a stay-at-home, as to give up some little thing to which one is attached.

The sacrifices of the body are not the most painful; there are the sacrifices of the soul, renunciation of self-love, readiness to submit to unjust or foolish judgments, suspicions, ridicule and the open or covert opposition of those whom one is trying to arouse to enthusiasm.

"I am not come to bring peace but the sword," said Jesus. And that is what He meant. In the same sense He said; "Behold I send you as sheep in the midst of wolves;" and "You shall be hated for my name's sake." "Christ is not come to be ministered unto but to minister, and to give his life a redemption for many." "Unless the grain of wheat falling into the ground die, itself remaineth alone. But if it die it bringeth forth much fruit."

It is childish to think that you can work for the advancement of the kingdom of God without encountering vigorous resistance. The brute in man always kicks against the message of Christ. Before the invitation of the spirit, the "sensual man," as St. Paul calls him,[3] shies and protests.

In the early days of Christianity when the faithful wanted to spread the reign of detachment, chastity and charity, men quickly sent for tigers and panthers to tear them to pieces in the amphitheaters, or else for a company of soldiers to cut off their

[3] I Cor. ii, 14.

heads. St. Paul tells us of the torments he had to undergo because he dared to preach the Gospel of Christ.[4] And there is not a single corner of the earth where the kingdom of our Saiviour has been founded without meeting resistance.

These texts and these facts are pregnant with meaning. To think that you can work for the salvation of the world without, directly or indirectly, partaking in the sacrifice of the Saviour of the world, is imagination pure and simple.

Our Lord was quite frank with His Apostles when He sent them forth on their mission: "Can you drink of the chalice which I shall drink?" He asked them; and only when they answered that they could, did He confide to them the task of saving their brethren.

Our Lord asks me too: "Can you drink of the chalice? Can you bear your part in your Master's sufferings?" What answer are we going to give? Shall we desert? Or shall we, like the Apostles, answer generously: "Yes, Lord, we can."

Sacrifice wins by force of example; and we

[4] 2 Cor. xi, 23.

have seen that Christ demanded it of those whom He had made His first Apostles. But there is a deeper reason which goes down to the roots of dogma. This reason has been explained elsewhere;[5] it will be enough to recall it here in a few words.

After original sin, by which the human race lost its divine life, Christ came to buy it back for us; but not as a benefactor who pays for us from without; He made us one with Him. He would be the one possessor of the divine life; but with Him we should be united as the members are united to the Head.

Now what method did Christ choose in order to ensure the salvation of the world? He taught men by His example and by His words, and that is why we too must exercise the apostolate by a faithful life and by courageous words. He prayed for souls; and that is why we must apostolize our brethren by praying for them. But the chief saving instrument is the Cross; and that is why, if we understand our mission as saviours of souls with Christ the Saviour, we must accept the cross and even seek it.

Christ might have saved the world with-

---

[5] See *In Christ Jesus* and *Christ in our brethren.* (Burns, Oates & Washbourne.)

out us. But He did not choose to do so. He deigned to will that we should make up what is wanting of the sufferings of Christ." Can anything be wanting to a sacrifice which is of infinite value? In itself, no. But in fact, Our Lord leaves us our part of the work to accomplish. The reason He has made us one with Him is in order that we may be able to pay our share. It is the *whole* Christ that must save the world; since I am one with Christ, since I am a living member of the whole Christ, I have a mission, a function to fulfill.

That is the essential word: a mission. Everyone who is baptized, if he understands the part he is to play, is a missionary. He may not be called upon to go to the heathens of Africa or Asia; his apostolate may be destined only to affect his near neighbours. But he must understand that wherever he may happen to be, there he has a function to perform: he has not only to save himself, but he has also to sanctify and save his brethren. And for that he needs example, certainly, like his Master; he needs words too; and certainly prayer. But above all, he needs the cross, sacrifice.

It remains to see now what this sacrifice may be.

CHAPTER III

THE SACRIFICES TO BE MADE

AMONG the various sacrifices that the apostle is called upon to make for the sanctification and salvation of his brethren, is the sacrifice of time.

There is great merit in encroaching upon the time which is destined for pleasure, rest and leisure; especially at an age when pleasure is of all things the most tempting. But let this be clearly understood: it is not a question of stealing hours or minutes from the duties of one's state. Before you think of busying yourself with your neighbour, even though it be to procure him the greatest benefit in the world (saving the case of his extreme need) you must give to God what He expects of you yourself.

Now those who seek to devote themselves to apostolic labours find that they are called upon to take part in a multitude of good works. And it sometimes happens that, to fulfill all their engagements, they have to dissipate their energies to the detriment of their apostolate, or else to neglect some important duty of their lives.

The great need is for unity and centralization. With so many different forms of activity being inaugurated every day it is difficult to see to which of them one ought to devote one's energies.

These various forms of apostolate are doubtless necessary in order to satisfy every taste. But let each man only undertake what he can frankly reconcile with his own state of life. Many would be well advised to undertake less, and the creators of new enterprises might well be asked whether there is not already in existence something of the same kind, or something very like it. If there is, then let them abstain. It is possible to have too much of a good thing.

If it is difficult to sacrifice one's time, it is still more difficult to sacrifice one's *reputation.*

A young man who devotes himself to the apostolate soon finds himself labelled; he finds himself regarded as a "weakling" or a hypocrite; he is called a "parson," or by some other amiably scornful name. And there is nothing that young men hate more than to be laughed at. Opposition or hatred they do not mind. But irony, there are few who have the courage to face it.

Let them remember the words of Our Lord to His Apostles: "You will be hated for my name's sake." It is all foreseen; and the apostle should know it: you cannot fight for Jesus Christ without risking sarcasm for the sake of Jesus Christ. Do not be afraid of it: pass it by.

Have we not many examples of men striving after a purely human ideal, who show the utmost contempt for what others may think of them? On his return from Rome Cardinal Liénart, addressing an audience of young men, quoted what the Holy Father had said to him about devotion to Soviet doctrine in Russia: "These people have an ideal. They are captivated by it. When necessary they are capable of suffering for it and even of risking their lives in defense of it. That is strength." The Pope added: "And, we, have we not a higher ideal? If we Catholics could be all captivated by that ideal to the extent of suffering something, and if necessary even risking our lives to realize it, then the victory would be ours."

We are not called upon to risk our lives: it

is simply a matter of facing a smile. Is the cause of Christ not worth that? At the beginning of every bold enterprise there have been men who scorned the sneers of scoffers. Were there not plenty of people to laugh at Christopher Columbus and his plans for discovering America, and more recently, at those who dreamed of ascending to the stratosphere by using the force of the tides? When the question of the Metro in Paris was first raised, crowds of jokers declared it impossible, and when the compressed air brake was discovered there were not lacking joyful prophets to declare that it was impossible to stop railway engines with wind. In 1894, a banquet was given to celebrate the first motor car to travel at 50 kilometers an hour, and André Michelin ventured to drink the health of "100 kilometers an hour." One of the diners said, in a voice loud enough to be heard by the proposer of the toast: "At the end of a dinner there is always somebody who has drunk too much and begins to talk nonsense."

• • • • •

Besides the sacrifice of time and the sacrifice of reputation, there is also *sacrifice*, simply, which is necessary in order to assure the triumph of the cause that we are defending.

There is, for example, the sacrifice of light or amusing books in favour of a deeper study which will give us a greater competence in our work and greater powers of conquest. A German chronicler of Soviet Russia has remarked how much struck he had been during his journeys across Siberia to notice that German, American or French travelers in the first or second-class carriages read only novels, while on the hard wooden benches of the third-class there were Russians, especially the young men, reading books on political economy and propaganda pamphlets.[1]

Then there is the sacrifice of a cigarette every day, so that at the end of the month you can pay your subscription, or help towards the creation of a sinking fund for the good of the cause. Here are some eloquent facts. In 1931 the tobacco monopoly yielded to the State 1600 millions more than in the preceding year. Statistics show that in the department of the Seine each citizen smokes 1097 cigarettes every year, and that

[1] Klaus Mehnert: *La Jeunesse en Russie soviétique*, p. 16.

is taking no count of those who smoke a pipe or make their own cigarettes. Elsewhere the figures vary, but they are still considerable. That means that each individual spends anything from 120 to 160 francs a year on tobacco. And yet we can complain sometimes that the treasurer asks too much, that he is always appealing to our pockets.

And what is a pipe or a cigarette, after all? A mere nothing. But it means so much: can I or can I not overcome myself? Can I restrain myself in little things like these? I have great ambitions, I aspire to great and generous sacrifices, I want to suffer for my Master, to carry the cross with Him . . . and I cannot even do this little thing. I am like the character described by Georges Duhamel in one of his novels: "He would give his life, but not this slice of mutton." That is just it.

My life God will probably not ask of me; what He would like me to give is just these little things. . . . "my slice of mutton," my 100 francs that go up in smoke. . . . I have not the courage to do it; and I think I am the stuff that apostles are made of!

However, we must be patient, we must train ourselves: we must make the beginning. "The threshold of the door," says a Danish proverb, "is the highest mountain in the world." It is true. It is not giving up smoking that is hard, it is the beginning of giving up smoking. Just as it is not difficult to pray; it is difficult to begin to pray. Beginnings are always difficult.

Admittedly, when the first step has been taken there still remains much to be done. Virtue necessarily presupposes not only the energy to undertake but also the generosity to persevere and the courage to accomplish. But it is a great deal to have begun. Indeed, well begun is half done; perhaps even three-quarters. At a meeting of young men a student thus addressed his companions:

"Where are these apostles coming from, these famous apostles who are going to change everything?"

". . . As soon as we have people who are real Christians and real men, then we shall have apostles.

"What sort of men do we want? Men capable of heroism even to the extent of shedding their blood? Yes, but first of all men who have courage enough to get out of bed in the morning when the bell rings. Men capable of putting into practice the ancient discipline of asceticism? Yes, but first of all men who have enough faith in the Redemption and the Eucharist to go to Mass sometimes during the week, and to go to communion more often than once a month, more often than every Sunday. Men capable of becoming missionaries of the gospel to the people? Yes, but first of all men who think of other things than dancing, riding, spending their evenings at bridge or wasting endless hours in cafés."

Each can examine and see on what points he ought to deny himself. The essential problem for each is: Do I want to be an apostle, yes or no? If you do, then go ahead. To his brother, Jerome, an indolent light-headed, easy-going man, Napoleon I addressed some severe remarks on the duty of a soldier and the duty of a sovereign:

"I have seen an order of the day emanating from you which has made you the laughing-stock of the whole of Germany, Austria and France. Have you not some friend, near you who can tell you a few truths? You are a King and a Brother of the Emperor: qualities which are simply ridiculous in war. You have to be a soldier, first, next, and all the time; you have to camp in the front line, be in the saddle day and night; or else remain in you seraglio. You fight like a satrap. Good heavens! Was it from me that you learned this? From me who, with an army of 200,000 men, am always at the head of my skirmishers. You have plent of pretentions, a little wit, a few good qualities, but all spoiled by foolishness and extreme presumption, and you have no knowledge of things. Fight like a young soldier who needs glory and reputation, and try to merit the rank you have attained.[2]

Change a few words and you can adapt this to your own case. If you want to be one of those who wins souls for Jesus Christ you must give up the life of a satrap, you must renounce an easy and comfortable existence. It is not from such that the salvation of the world will come.

Happy those who have been educated to sacrifice by a manly upbringing: "My mother always brought me up to conquer myself and gradually to overcome myself more and more. 'You have to become a man, Francis,' she said, 'not a bedraggled chicken; and you

---

[2] Arthur Lévy: *Les dissentiments de la famille impériale.*

can do it.' She trained me to self-restraint from the age of three or four years. 'Would you like to try drinking your coffee without sugar, or eating your bread without butter? It is Advent (or Lent). Try, won't you? Just to see if you can. It will be an economy and you can give the money to this poor sick person.'"

"Later when I went to school: 'Go out with your money in your pocket and see the shops in the fair, with the sweets and the rest. Don't buy anything, and tomorrow give your threepence to Jacob, or to old Joseph. A boy ought to be able to say "no" to his desires, and say it with a smile and a whistle.' and she set us the example."

"When we fought with other boys: 'You will leave Michael alone to-morrow. He may have acted like a blackguard. But, you see, he has no one to bring him up properly. Go on your way and don't touch him. The silliest young boys can insult others, that is much more difficult.

"Later it was the same. 'To go about with girls and do as everybody else does is easy enough. The silliest coxcomb can do that. But you have to remain pure. Be polite to all girls, as if they were your sisters, but do not be affectionate with any, until it is a question of marrying. Don't waste your virility, so that you may be able one day to beget fine children, full of health and hope for the future. A man goes straight on his path without hesitation; he obeys his inner conviction . A poor vacillating "good fellow" merely goes with the crowd.' "[3]

Those who have not received such a manly education must give it to themselves. They must, in the words of Claudel, "make acquaintance with iron and steel, they must learn the healthy athletic joys of self-conquest." And so that this programme may have an apostolic bearing, keep in mind the words of Jacques d'Arnoux: "Sacrifices are the jewels that God gives you in order to save your brethren. In return you give him only gravel; you are a coiner. To give these diamonds their infinite value resignation is not sufficient. Come, take advantage of the days of prosperity to give alms to the poor and sorrowful. Waste nothing; give everything. Be munificent."

[3] Quoted by Lisberg Burger: *Mémoires d'une sage-femme,* pp. 120-21. The youth in question was Gonzague de Geloes, buried in the Visitation chapel at Annécy. He joined as a volunteer in 1916 and died in 1918 at the age of nineteen.

We are told in the book of Exodus that when Moses was commanded by God to build the tabernacle, the Israelites brought and laid before the feet of the prophet gold and silver, bronze, purple dyes, linen, flocks, woods of all kinds, oil, perfumes and various sorts of stones. Of all these the Lord would make a tabernacle, He said, and He would dwell in the midst of them.[4]

If the temple of Christianity is to be built, every apostle must make his plentiful contribution of generous sacrifice. The offerings may be varied; it is desirable that they should. Upon their number and their quality depends the building of the Kingdom of God.

[4] Exod. xxv, 3-8.

BOOK IV

"et sepultus est."

BURIAL

CHAPTER I

THE MASTER'S EXAMPLE

THERE is a thing more terrible than dying, and that is being buried; I mean being buried alive.

To take part in the work of Redemption means following the Master even to that length. *Descendit; Incarnatus est; Passus; Sepultus est.* He came down from heaven, became incarnate, died and was buried.

But, you will say, Jesus was not buried alive when He was taken down from the Cross. Agreed; and it is not of the burial which immediately followed Calvary that we would speak, though the symbolical value of this is not to be neglected; but we mean here anther burial by which Jesus was buried alive: His burial as the Word, together with the Father and the Holy Ghost, in the soul of men by sanctifying grace; or His burial as the Word Incarnate in our tabernacles.

Is it not characteristic of the divine activity that the more completely the immediate agent is hidden, the more completely that power is displayed?

Should we ever have thought of this as the most effective means by which God could act upon men: that He should imprison Himself for twenty-four hours out of every twenty-four, in the innumerable tombs of our tabernacles, unknown and forgotten; that He should shut Himself up in the heart of man, and there, unknown and unfelt, move His will, enlighten His mind, and give a divine orientation to His activity?

How discreet is this buried God within us! It would seem that He fears to frighten us by too manifest a presence, that He fears to impose Himself upon our wills in such a way as to diminish the freedom of our consent. So delicate, so discreet is His action that when, afterwards, we try to point to the exact moment in which that divine action began we often find it impossible to do so. It is the triumph of the imperceptible.

The lesson of all this is clear enough: in order to act upon our souls God buries Himself.

After all, what did Our Lord achieve during His *visible* ministry and by His exterior action among men? Little or nothing. The Apostles did not understand Him, or if they did, very imperfectly. The multitude demanded miracles, cried "Hosanna" one day and "Give us Barabbas" the next. The leaders of the people were alarmed, then suspicious, and finally they crucified Him.

It is when the Master disappears from sight that the dawn of the Redemption breaks. "When the Son of Man shall be raised up from the earth, then He will draw all things to himself."

But—forgive me, Lord, if I appear to correct you—when you were raised up from the earth what did you draw to yourself? Very little, it would seem! The Apostles all run away, the soldiers play their game of dice, the multitude depart from Golgotha shaking their heads, Herod continues his festivities. Only the centurion recognizes you: "Of a truth this man was the Son of God." The centurion, besides two women and John. Not a very great victory!

Ah, Lord, I know that you spoke of the times which were to come until the end of the world. And you spoke also of the end-

125

less renewal of the sacrifice of the cross by the sacrifice of the Mass. But even so, would it not have been more true to say: "When I am buried the world will awake. When I have disappeared they will see me. When I am laid in the earth the flowers will come forth?" Did you not say yourself: "Unless the grain of wheat falling into the ground die, itself remaineth alone. But if it die it bringeth forth much fruit?"

But forgive me, Lord. I seem to be trying to teach You whereas it is I that have everything to learn.

"I am not offended, My son. What you are trying to say contains a salutary truth, and I am not loth that you should seek, however gropingly, to find it. What you say is true: the great secret of a fruitful apostolate is to be buried. The most successful apostles are not those that make the greatest show, and the best successes are not those that are most apparent. The most solid articles in a review are not always those which are signed by great names; a page may be excellent, and yet its author unknown. Was not the war won more by 'unknown soldiers' than by men whose names history will cherish? In the history of the salvation of souls much might be written concerning the success of failures and the vicissitudes of retarded successes. It would make interesting and surprising reading.

"Look at my own failures! You mentioned some of them just now. And how many others there are! Do you think I was very successful with Judas? Did the young man who came to Me full of ardour and zeal, seeking a life of perfection, did he, think you, follow My advice? No, he went away sorrowful, and the Gospel loses all traces of him. When I foretold the Eucharist to the Jews, you might have thought that they would have thrown themselves at My feet in gratitude. On the contrary: 'These words are hard, and who can bear them?' That was the response of a great number of them. And the ingratitude of the lepers that were cleansed and the paralytics that were cured; and the narrow outlook even of those who were very close to Me!

"But have patience. A building cannot rise until great numbers of stones have been buried in the earth to give it a foundation. Think of Lisieux, and the hill upon which the basilica stands. Think of the rubble that had to be buried before even the smallest wall could rise above the soil. Plans had been made. But hard facts caused the plans to be changed; the soil was unstable, it was slipping. Tons of concrete had to be poured in, otherwise nothing would have held. Souls, too, are so unstable; who shall tell the generosity that has to be poured into their foundations before they decide to hold fast?

"Yes, one day, at the hour fixed by My Providence, a tower, a temple, a basilica is seen to arise. In the days when it took hundreds of years to build a cathedral, do you think that the architect of the early beginnings ever saw the completion of his plan? The man who lays the foundation stone is not always the man that lays the top stone of the pinnacle. And it is better so. If every sower, whether sowers of cathedrals or sowers of souls, saw the completion of his work, he might perhaps be too proud. I save them from this danger.

"Sometimes it is even worse. Solid foundations have been laid. And yet on those foundations either nothing will be built, or else something will be built entirely different from what the founder planned. This is pleasing to Me: complete generosity and complete humility. Apparently nothing has been raised above the soil. But I do not need those who raise, I need those who hide themselves. From generous zeal that has been buried in one corner of a field I can raise up wonders of grace in the opposite corner. In the invisible world what is apparently of no use at all is often that which serves the best. A failure, well accepted by an apostle who has displayed all his energy to succeed, is more salutary than many a triumph. The triumph might have occasioned a little pride. Humility is pure gold; and with that money the debt of many can be paid.

"And so, My son, cast your seed tirelessly. Be not solicitous what may become of it. 'Sow the seed,' said a holy soul,[1] 'without looking to see where it falls.' Zeal with detachment, that is what is needed. No ostentation, no outward show: *sepultus*. Go even further, and thank God in advance for the apostolic results of your failures. That will be a good act of faith. Perhaps what happened to Me will happen

---

[1] Marie-Antionette de Geuser. In her *Life* (published by the A. de la P., Toulouse), are to be found valuable counsels on the matter of the apostolate, given by her to her brother, at that time a Jesuit novice.

also to you. When I spoke to that man, he would not understand Me; but how many young men in the course of ages will recall My words to him! It was a failure; but what a success withal! And you know how they murmured and went away when I spoke to them of the Eucharist. But see how many since then have come to Me, hungry for the living Bread. It was a check; but what a triumph, too!

"The same will happen to you. You will speak; and at the moment you will not be heard. But later one of your hearers whose heart had been closed will open it. You will act; at the moment your zeal will be still-born. But some day, when you do not know it, some soul will be touched and will receive life through you. Be thankful in anticipation for this delayed and obscure success.[2]

---

[2] When P. Olivaint died under the Commune it was a woman wearing a military cap—Louise Gimet, "Captain Pigerre"—that fired the fatal shot. "Madame" the Jesuit had said to her, "that costume does not suit you." She had fired at him point-blank. Subsequently, at St. Lazare she was given a book to keep her quiet. It was the sermons of the man she had killed. Through the reading of these she was enlightened by grace. Did Olivaint suspect, when he published that book, that it would convert his murderess? (Mme Ancelet-Hustache: *Les soeurs des Prisons*. Grasset, p. 140.)

"There, my son, are a few lessons, among many that I might give. They will no doubt change your view of the apostolate. Never mind. Believe me; in the science of the salvation of the world I speak what I know. You tell Me that you want to be a redeemer of the world. Good; I congratulate you. Well, that is how redemption is accomplished."

My Lord, I hear you, and I will use your precious lessons in the work of my youthful apostolate. Saviours come forth from the tomb. Teach me to bury myself.

CHAPTER II

HOW TO BURY MYSELF

LET us recall what has been said before: it is not his own cause that the apostle promotes and defends, but God's. His zeal must never puff him up. St. John the Baptist said: "He must increase and I must decrease." St. Paul goes further. He must not only decrease, he must disappear altogether. "I live, now not I; but Christ it is that liveth in me."

Hence the important consequence: we must avoid as the plague any jealousy of those who are working with us and who have better success than we.

One day the Apostles were going with Jesus to Capharnaum, and they were a little advance of Him, deep in some discussion. On their arrival at the village, Jesus, who had noticed their animated conversation, asked them: "What did you treat of in the way?" The poor Apostles held their peace, being covered with shame, "for in the way they had disputed among themselves which of them should be the greatest."[1]

To submit with a good grace to being the least, not to sound one's own trumpet, not to mind being an apparently insignificant cog in the machinery, to leave the best, or at any rate the most important, part to others, is the ABC of the hidden apostolate. There are many who never succeed in deciphering these elementary letters, and they remain forever beginners.

It is a curious thing to see how many great works have no known signature. What a number of cathedrals there are whose architect is unknown! How many famous paintings, sculptures, writings, inventions there are, of which we shall never know who was the genius that brought them out of the Limbo of nothingness!

Take for example the brazen disk under the Arc de Triomphe from which the flame issues that celebrates the memory of the unknown soldier. Is there anybody who has not seen it? But ask the passers-by if they know the name of the man who first thought of the idea, who first planned it, or the name

[1] Mark ix, 32 ff.

of the metal-worker who executed it?[2] Nobody knows. It is not only the unknown soldier that lies buried under the Arc de Triomphe; together with him are buried those who have striven to sing his praises.

And there are countries which have been discovered and which do not bear the name of the first man to land on them. Christopher Columbus was the first to conceive the idea of going in search of the New World; but it was not he, but Americo Vespucci, a Florentine, who set out upon a second expedition, that unwittingly gave his name to the newly discovered continent.

The Queen of Spain had promised ten thousand maravedis (about eight thousand francs) to the first seaman under the command of Columbus who should sight the coast they sought. The leader of the expedition had himself promised the fortunate man a silken doublet. Vain offers; not a name has come down to posterity. We do not know who was the first to see America.

[2] As a matter of fact, the original idea was to have a tripod. But this would have spoiled the perspective. It was the architect Henry Favier, a modest man who has produced many works of art which do not bear his hame, that first suggested the plan which was subsequently adopted.

And if this is the case with human affairs and enterprises, it is much more so with the affairs and enterprises of God. Discoveries and institutions remain. The discoverers, the creators and the institutors are often unknown, or else they have soon fallen into oblivion. Such is the triumph of hidden zeal.

• • • • •

The second important thing for the apostle to remember is that he must not allow himself to be disappointed if the work upon which he has set his heart ends in failure. The generous acceptance of failure in advance does much to promote the cause of God. God wants virtue rather than triumphs. And who knows but that an apparent failure may prove to be a real triumph, though it may remain hidden? God, who lives in an eternal present, may, in a far off place at some remote time, grant graces which had otherwise been refused.

Put into the foundations of the work all the effort you can, intelligent and detached effort: "Never give up until you have tried everything," Foch used to say. But when you have done that, acknowledge that you have done nothing, and that grace alone can bring the work to fruition.

135

Have boundless trust in God. Many generous efforts come to nothing because there has been too much self-confidence. Count only on God. Live by faith. Believe in the omnipotence and infinite subtlety of grace. What Peguy said is quite true: "Grace is insidious, grace is cunning and unexpected. It is as obstinate as a woman, and like a woman it is tenacious, and clinging. Put it out at the window and it will enter by the door. The men that God wants to have, He has. The humanities that God wants to have, He has. The humanity that Jesus wanted to have, God's grace gave to Him. When grace does not come directly, it comes indirectly. When it does not come from the right, it is coming from the left. When it does not come straight, it is because it is coming on a curve; and when it does not come on a curve, it is because it is coming in bits. When it wants somebody, it has him. It does not take the same roads that we do; it takes its own. It does not even take its own, for it never takes the same road twice. When it does not come from above, it is because it it is coming from below; and when it does not come from the centre, it is because it is coming from the circumference. And the water of this spring, when it does not come forth as from a gushing fountain, may trickle like the water that oozes under the dykes of the Loire."

If grace is the most important character in the drama of the sanctification and salvation of souls, it follows that the apostle is only a minor actor, necessary indeed, because God has willed it so, but one whose place is more behind the scenes than on the stage. He is there to change the general appearance of things to allow God to vary His technique, and to bring about the victorious ending in a different way.

Remember that though grace is powerful it is slow in its action. God could work quickly if He willed. He chooses not to. He has the whole of eternity at His disposal. When the farmer has sown his seed in the furrow he does not come out the next morning to see whether it has grown yet. No, he knows that the seed takes time to germinate. It make take weeks, or even months. Apostles, especially young apostles are always in a hurry: they want to see the harvest the day after the seed has been sown. You do not convert a soul or a group of souls quickly. "You cannot bear them now," said Our Lord one day to His Disciples. You cannot now understand what I am preaching to you; but you will later. Have patience.

But precisely because you are willing not to hurry matters, you will have confidence in the future. One of the most necessary qualities for an apostle is "a sense of the future"; that is, to be able not only to wait patiently, but also foresee the method that will be necessary in order to reach souls more effectively.

Napoleon is supposed to have said: "I only live two years ahead."

A professor of Philosophy[3] in taking leave of his pupils made the following commentary upon the parable of the wise and foolish virgins:

"They fell asleep while awaiting the bridegroom and they are condemned to follow him from afar, carrying their empty lamps. What a beautiful symbol! How many there are that spend their whole lives following after an event, always to late for it because they have fallen asleep waiting for it. Mark well, the event will come like a thief, and you must await it with eyes open and with lamps burning." He added: "It is

---

[3] Alain Chartier. See Massis: *Jugements.*

not enough to live on the dreams of the day before yesterday; we must have a thought also for to-morrow."

Abbé de Tourville gave the same advice in more vigorous terms: "Let us live in the present like men that have come from the future. . . . What we are to-day in small numbers, people will be in great numbers at no very distant time. We are like people of the twenty-second century who have been given the mission of conquering the twentieth; we have to stoop to these old men and engraft upon them the youth of the future.

"One of our trials is that we see the good more clearly than others. You will say that the good is clear in itself, and that everybody ought to see it. I agree; but remember that Christopher Columbus did not succeed in making people understand his plan. And yet there was no malice in them. In other matters, besides the discovery of America, we find the same sort of foolishness in varying degrees. But it must be admitted that it is much more common to-day."

The same author writes: "In every period of history God sets precursors who either act or think in the future. It is a great blessing for them to live in advance of their times, though it means that they live alone. Abraham had this good fortune, when he desired to see, and saw the days of Christ more than 1500 years before he came."[4]

To have within yourself, buried deep down, a clear view of all that must be done if the future is to be as Christ requires it to be, and this not merely in general but in detail; and despite misunderstandings, opposition, and contradiction, despite the inner distaste that all such antagonisms cause, to make hidden but effective preparations for the times that are to come-what a task! But what a glorious task!

A humorist said of a certain politician: "His misfortune is that he knows history; and so he lives in a cometary."

No; we must not despise the past, still less must we be ignorant of it. We must neglect nothing that may serve to give us a better understanding of the present and of the organization which is necessary for the future. Thank God, it is possible to know history, and yet not live in a cometary.

But more than the past, what we have to learn to know—so that we may make it as

[4]*La piété confiante*, pp. 163-164.

we want it to be—is the future. Rightly or wrongly, the clergy of France have been reproached for not foreseeing 1789, the clergy of Spain for not foreseeing the popular movement of 1931, the Russian clergy with not foreseeing Lenin and his party. If that reproach is justified, it is unfortunate. Let it be a lesson for the future.

However that may be, a modern author thinks that it is our duty to see that we do not too often remain behind the events of the day. According to him, a certain habit of mind makes us inclined to do so. This is what he says:

"Catholics for the most part defend tradition and defend it ably; and this is one of the reasons of the formidable power of the church; but concerning recent developments they are reserved and skeptical. Hence if it is a question of combating false ideas or resisting dangerous innovations, Catholicism is a most valuable weight on the other side of the balance. But that same conservatism is a hindrance when it is a question of raising up leaders, of finding men who will foster creative action and encourage progress. Here Catholicism allows itself to be pushed too far into the background. Subsequently it will take the right path. But then it will only be playing the part of a tolerated disciple."[5]

Let us never forget: we have ourselves to live—and we have to help other souls to live—a life without end, but a life which on this earth is set in a particular period of time; it is therefore of the highest importance that we should understand the times that are coming. Otherwise we run the risk of being out of date, incapable of influencing our own age, through lack of comprehensiveness, lack of foresight, lack of adaptability.

It may be that we shall die with our dream still buried in our hearts. But at least we shall have lived in a manner which makes life worth living.

Moreover, have we not the Church to help us in our imperfect comprehension of the future? She is believed to be exclusively preoccupied with Tradition. But she is just as much, if not more, preoccupied with the Future. It is for us, her children, not to defy her directions when she gives them, but to accept them and under her guidance to

[5] Rademaker: *Religion et Vie,* p. 279. (Bruxelles, éd. *La Cité Chrétienne,* 1934.)

march boldly ahead.

It may mean giving up some of our opinions, renouncing some of our dreams. Then let us bury ourselves by burying them carefully; and welcome the judgments, decisions and directions of our Mother the Church.

CONCLUSION

THERE are many who lament that the world fares ill today. Has there ever been a time when you think it fared well? Doubtless sometimes it has fared better, sometimes worse; and you are at liberty to think that this is one of the "worse" moments. But what is the use of lamenting? It does no good. Rather let us say: If the world fares ill, then so much the more work for us to do if we want it to fare well.

Saving the world has never been an easy task. It was not easy for the Son of God. It was not easy for His Apostles. But He is with us. And that brings us back to the confidence of our beginning. Under such a leader, is there any limit to what soldiers may do, soldiers full of zeal and resolution, trained in His methods?

Mecum. You are with Me. And I have overcome the world. He does not speak of the future: "I will overcome the world ." He uses the past tense: "I have overcome." One thing only is wanting to make this the present tense: my active, understanding and

144

intelligent collaboration. When all the other Christs have decided to help Christ, then Redemption through Christ will be fully accomplished.

Let us pray that apostles may come, and that they may be such as the world and God require them to be.

Many new & exciting releases for 1998

(If you are interested in any or all of these exciting new titles send us your name and address and we can send you a notice of publication with the price.)

By Way of the Cross
By Carol J. Ross—Autobiography. When you read By Way of the Cross you will open yourself to tears of empathy and of joy as you see this woman struggling with terribly physical and mental crosses, scooped up into breathtaking visions of the supernatural world. Paperback. Full color photos. 468 pages. *Price $12.25 each*

Lost in the World: Found in Christ
By Father Christopher Scadron—The story of a priest ordained at the age of 63 — As a young Jewish man Padre Pio predicated he would become a Priest. After years of floundering and sin as a naval officer and an artist, this unsually gifted and interesting man became a priest at 63! A tale all Catholics will find moving and deeply inspiring, it is also a must gift for any man you know who might be called to the priesthood at an age older than the usual. *Price $12.50 each*

Dancing with God through the Evening of Life
By Mary Anne McCrickard Benas—Unique insight into the world of the hospice worker and the patient relationship. The beautiful faithful outlook of a elderly man dying and the gifts he gives us through this experience. *Price $12.50 each*

The Third Millennium Woman
By Patricia Hershwitzky—Consider the sinking feeling many Catholics get when they see literature about preparing for this great event. They expect what they read or pretend to read to be true, but dull as dishwater. By contrast — here is a book that is wildly funny and also profound.

Written by a "revert" (born Catholic who left and then returned), it is also ideal as a gift for those many women we know are teetering on the verge of returning Home.

Messages to the World from the Mother of God
Daily meditative pocketsize prayer book on the monthly messages given the visionaries in Medjugorje for the conversion of the World, back to her son Jesus. These messages for the World started in 1984 till the present. In 1987 the messages began on the 25th of the month (union of two hearts with the 5 wounds of Jesus) thus the 25th. These are from St. James Church in Medjugorje. Great Gift!!! *Price $10.00 each*

Children of the Breath
By Martin Chervin—Who would have dared to challenge Creation if, at the close of each new day, God said, "It is perfect." Instead, His lips spoke "It is good . . ." and the serpent was already in Eden. Thus begins Children of the Breath, a startling journey into the desert where Christ was tempted for forty days of darkness and light. With immense clarity, lyricism, and humor, author Martin Chervin has delivered a powerhouse that will engage readers of any faith.

Behold the Man, Simon of Cyrene
By Father Martin DePorres—Inspired writing by a gifted new Author. This story shows us the gifts given to Simon. Through carrying the Cross with Jesus, Simon shares with us the gifts we can expect by carrying our daily crosses. *Price $12.25 each*

Becoming the Handmaid of the Lord
By Dr. Ronda Chervin—The journals of this well known Catholic writer span her family life as wife and mother, mystical graces sustaining her through a mid-life crisis, the suicide of her beloved son, her widowhood and finally a Religious Sister at the age of 58. Insightful, inspiring & challenging. 327 pages of the heart. *Price $13.75 each*

Ties that Bind
By Ronda Chervin—The story of a Marriage. This beautiful novel presents the wife's point of view and the husbands point of view on the same conflict. The author Dr. Chervin has written many books on Catholic life. Ties that Bind is both funny and inspiring. A great gift for couple thinking about marriage as well. *Price $8.50 each*

The Cheese Stands Alone
By David Craig—(The formost religious poet of the day) A dynamite account of a radical conversion from the world of drugs to the search for holiness in the Catholic Church. Realism & poetic imagery combine to make this a must for those who want the real thing. Its a rare book that both monastic and charismatic — anyone acquainted with the latter will love the chapter on misguided zeal, aptly titled "Busbey Burkeley." *Price $12.50 each*

The History of Eucharistic Adoration
By Father John Hardon, S.J.—In an age of widespread confusion and disbelief, this document offers unprecedented clarity in the most important element of our faith. I recommend that it be prayerfully studied and widely circulated. It is thoroughly researched and well documented, and promises to enlight en, instruct and inspire countless souls to an undying love of our Eucharistic Lord.
Price $4.00 each

The Bishop Sheen We Knew
By Father Albert Shamon—A booklet filled with little known information from his Vicar, Fr. Albert J.M. Shamon, Bishop Dennis Hickey and Fr. Mike Hogan, the three remaining priests who worked under Bishop Sheen. A chance to see the day to day workings of the acknowledged prophet of our times. *Price $4.00 each*

Becoming a Woman of God—Each week of this unique journal centers on a provocative theme concerning topics relating to women. Each day offers a quotation as well as a short teaching or exercise. Jouirnal space is provided on each day for the reader to include her responses. Can be shared in groups. *Price $9.95 each*

Freed to Love—Freed to Love offers healing for women through prayer, witness, Catholic teaching and meditation. Topics include abuse, post-abortion syndrome, divorce and importance of Mary in healing. The book has been popular in workshops around the world. *Price $6.95 each*

The Fabric of Our Lives—A compendium of short stories based on fabrics woven into a literary quilt. The stories cover every phase of a woman's life from childhood to grandmotherhood, combining the wit, pathos, and eloquence of twenty authors. *Price $13.95 each*

The Right Way to Live—Looking for a book for yourself and others that proves there are moral absolutes? Here is a highly readable, humorous but incisive approach endorsed by leading scholars. *Price $12.95 each*

Voyage to Insight—Are you a Catholic looking for a book to help your non-Christian friends to find Truth. This imaginative approach to finding your own philosophy of life enables the reader to dialogue with great thinkers as he or she inserts personal ideas into the book. *Price $12.95 each*

To order additional copies of this book:

Please complete the form below and send to:
CMJ Associates, Inc.
P.O. Box 661
Oak Lawn, IL 60454
call 708-636-2995 or fax 708-636-2855
email jwby@aol.com

Name _____

Address _____

City _____

State_____ Zip _____

Phone (   )_____

Book Name		Quantity	Subtotal
Radiating Christ			
(price $11.00)	x		=
_____	x		=
_____	x		=
+ tax (for Illinois residents only)		=	
shipping & handling		=	
Total			

☐ Check # _____   ☐ Visa   ☐ MasterCard

Exp. Date _____

Card # _____

Signature _____